SINATRA
YOU TO K
EVEN HE
THE POWER TO KEEP YOU
FROM FINDING OUT ABOUT:

—What his childhood in Hoboken was *really* like, as opposed to the sentimental PR version

—The story told of how a gun was put to Tommy Dorsey's head to release Sinatra from a contract

—How Sinatra was a step away from suicide when his chance to act in *From Here to Eternity* saved him

—How Sinatra discovered the singing secret that put him on top

—The night that Marilyn Monroe tried to offer herself naked to Sinatra and his poker-playing buddies

And everything else, including the wives, the lovers, the friends, the enemies, the notorious "acquaintances," the charities, the vendettas, the triumphs, the disasters, the scandals, and, above all, through it all, the incredible musicianship.

SINATRA
The Man and the Myth

SINATRA

The Man and The Myth

*AN UNAUTHORIZED
BIOGRAPHY*

by
Bill Adler

A SIGNET BOOK

NEW AMERICAN LIBRARY

PUBLISHED BY
THE NEW AMERICAN LIBRARY
OF CANADA LIMITED

NAL BOOKS ARE AVAILABLE AT QUANTITY DISCOUNTS
WHEN USED TO PROMOTE PRODUCTS OR SERVICES.
FOR INFORMATION PLEASE WRITE TO PREMIUM MARKETING DIVISION,
NEW AMERICAN LIBRARY, 1633 BROADWAY,
NEW YORK, NEW YORK 10019.

First Printing, March, 1987

2   3   4   5   6   7   8   9

SIGNET TRADEMARK REG U S PAT OFF AND FOREIGN COUNTRIES
REGISTERED TRADEMARK — MARCA REGISTRADA
HECHO EN WINNIPEG, CANADA

SIGNET, SIGNET CLASSIC, MENTOR, ONYX, PLUME, MERIDIAN
AND NAL BOOKS are published in Canada by The New American
Library of Canada, Limited, 81 Mack Avenue, Scarborough,
Ontario, Canada M1L 1M8
PRINTED IN CANADA
COVER PRINTED IN U.S.A.

Contents

Contents

★ 1 ★

The Maggio Connection

It was an odd place for a duel, this sumptuous suite at the Hampshire House in New York. Through the windows you could see the lush green of Central Park, bathed in the sunshine of a bright blue sky.

While what was going on was indeed a duel, it was an intellectual duel, a duel of egos, a duel of truths and half truths. It was a duel to the death for one of the participants, and a duel for professional survival for the other.

The man who held the upper hand was one of Hollywood's most loved and hated legends. Variously known as King Cohn, Harry the Horror, and White Fang, Harry Cohn was the head of one of the motion picture business's most prestigious studios. Determinedly uncouth and outlandish in his manner, Cohn was actually a shrewd observer and arbiter of public taste.

With a poverty row studio that pinched pennies and drew up tight contracts with performers of all kinds, Cohn at Columbia Pictures had come up with such Golden Age classics as *It Happened One Night, The Awful Truth,* and *All the King's Men.* Now he had purchased a property that he thought might become another classic of the industry: *From Here to Eternity,* James Jones's monumental World War II saga.

Cohn was at the pinnacle of his power and clout.

The man opposite him was everything that Cohn was *not.* Frank Sinatra had achieved meteoric success in the chaotic world of popular music. Emerging at a time when Bing Crosby was leading the pack and winning all the awards, Sinatra had partly modeled himself after Crosby, but at the same time had developed his own individual style. He *used* the microphone to project his voice and with its help created a style that had made him the hero of every teenage girl in America.

As fast as fame had come to him during the World War II years, it had begun to slip away from him in the early 1950s. Sinatra, who like Harry Cohn had many monikers—one of them was The Voice—had slipped from the peak of his popularity and begun a precipitous slide back into obscurity.

ITEM: His weekly radio show, *The Frank Sinatra Hour,* had just been canceled.

ITEM: The film offers that he had always managed to get throughout his short career had now dried up.

ITEM: His nightclub engagements, the source of most of his income, had peaked and those that he got were now second-rate.

ITEM: He owed the Internal Revenue Service over $100,000 in back taxes.

ITEM: News of his earlier association with Mafia dons—especially the notorious Lucky Luciano—had tarnished his image with the public.

ITEM: He had begun to indulge in fistfights in public places with journalists—notably Lee Mortimer of the Hearst chain.

ITEM: He had divorced his first wife and married screen siren Ava Gardner, whose path was upward while Sinatra's was downward.

ITEM: His wife Ava was now scheduled to fly to Africa to make a film with Clark Gable and Grace Kelly, while Sinatra was scrounging for work around the fringes of the entertainment world.

ITEM: Sinatra was broke. Ava was earning the family bread. It was a galling thing to be a nonworking husband to a working wife.

There was one bright spot in all the gloom, however. Sinatra had read *From Here to Eternity* and was fascinated by it. Mostly he was entranced by the character of Private Angelo Maggio, a fast-talking Italian barracks-room rebel who is finally beaten to death in the stockade because of his unquenchable spirit. Intuitively, Sinatra knew that this was *the* role in the movie. He felt that if he could get the part, he would immediately be on the comeback trail. But if he didn't . . .

Because he had no immediate work in view, Sinatra had agreed to travel to Africa with his wife for the filming of *Mogambo,* a remake of MGM's old hit *Red Dust.* Staying a few days at the Hampshire House on Central Park South, he learned through the grapevine that Harry Cohn was registered at the same hotel. So Sinatra inveigled his way into Cohn's suite to tackle White Fang in his expensive lair.

That meeting's conversation has been told in many versions, their differences depending on the writer's attitude toward Sinatra. It probably went something like this:

SINATRA: Harry, I want to play Maggio.
COHN: You must be out of your fucking mind!
SINATRA: No, Harry.
COHN: This is an actor's part. Not a crooner's.

Sinatra kept his peace; he knew Cohn was trying to shake him up and throw him off rhythm. If he blew up, he knew Cohn could dismiss him as a crackpot and throw him out of the suite. Sinatra sweetened up and became the wheedling street operator that he had learned to be as a youth on the Hoboken docks.

SINATRA: Harry, you've known me for a long time.
COHN: Yeah.
SINATRA: This part was written about a guy like me.
COHN: (Unconvinced) Uh-huh.
SINATRA: I'm an actor!
COHN: Come on, Frank! You're a crooner—nothing else but!
SINATRA: Give me a *chance* to act. I'll act your pants off.

Cohn sat there, his entire physiognomy radiating indifference. Inside his mind, however, the wheels were turning.

Unknown to Sinatra, the role of Maggio had already been cast by the picture's director, Fred Zinnemann, its script writer, Daniel Taradash, and its producer, Buddy Adler. Maggio was to be played by Eli Wallach, the well-known Broadway actor. But even among the picture's top production executives, a problem was developing.

While Zinnemann wanted Wallach in the role, Taradash had reservations—not about Wallach's acting, but about his physical appearance. He seemed to be too much on top of things, both physically and psychologically. Could he get that vulnerability, that hint of desperation, that quality of doom, that the actor who played Maggio had to project?

Sinatra read Cohn's expression exactly as Cohn wanted him to read it.

SINATRA: Harry, I'll pay *you* to let me play the role!
COHN: You're nuts! You're a song-and-dance man. Maggio is stage-actor kind of stuff.

Sinatra decided now that he had *not* been wasting his time. When he had said he would pay Cohn to do the role, he saw a wild glint in the old skinflint's eye.

SINATRA: About the money . . .
COHN: Who's talking money? (Short pause) What *about* the money?

Sinatra knew what a cheapie Cohn was; he also knew that in the gambling dens of Las Vegas Cohn dropped money wildly. He knew Cohn loved to flash a thick roll around. Money was a principal consideration with him, even if he liked to pretend it wasn't.

"I've been getting a hundred and fifty thousand a film," Sinatra went on airily.

"You *used* to get a hundred and fifty thousand," Cohn corrected him.

"All right. I *used* to get it. But do you know what I'll play Maggio for?"

Now there was a silence while Cohn's eyes drilled into Sinatra's. Sinatra could tell he was thinking. But Cohn didn't want Sinatra to *know* he was thinking. That meant he might be weakening in his opposition.

COHN: I'm not buying, Frank. (Pause) But just for the record, what's the fancy price?

Sinatra knew he had him. He waited a long time before he finally came out with it. He could see Cohn's eyes watching him carefully, brightly. He would have played the part for nothing, just as he had already told Cohn kiddingly, but that would cheapen him in Cohn's eyes.

SINATRA: I'm not kidding, Harry. You can get Maggio for . . .

Cohn said nothing. The silence intensified.

SINATRA: . . . a thousand a week.

Now Sinatra could see Cohn multiplying the numbers in his head. A thousand dollars times eight, the number of weeks in the tight shooting schedule. The answer: eight thousand bucks!

Cohn looked out the window. "You want it that much, Frank?"

6

"I've got to have it. It was written for me—for *me* and nobody else."

Sinatra knew when to end a scene. He stood up. It was all over. He walked toward the door. He had given it his best shot. Had he failed? Or . . .

As the door opened, Cohn's mouth opened. "Well, we'll see, Frank. We'll see. Meanwhile, we've got some other actors—regular actors—to test."

Sinatra hid a triumphant smile. It was a reprieve! It was a goddamned reprieve!

SINATRA: You're not turning me down, then?
COHN: I'll think it over. It's pretty crazy.
SINATRA: I won't let you down!

Shortly after returning to his own suite, Sinatra was called to the telephone. It was Cohn's office in Los Angeles.

"Mr. Cohn says he's going to give you a chance to have a screen test for the role of Private Angelo Maggio in *From Here to Eternity*," a voice told him.

That was typical Cohn. Telephone from New York to his office to have his office phone back to New York for Sinatra—when he was about fifteen yards away.

"When?" Sinatra asked.

"We'll call you," the voice said sweetly, and the connection was broken.

Sinatra's spirits were up as he joined his wife Ava to fly to Africa for *Mogambo*. But once he was there, his optimism collapsed when, several days later, he read that Eli Wallach was being considered for the role of Maggio. Of course the item had been leaked to the press, as such things always are, to publicize the coming production. However, the way the leak was worded led Sinatra to believe that Wallach had already been selected and had perhaps even been signed.

What Sinatra did not know was that Cohn had budgeted $16,000 for the role of Maggio, and was presently haggling with Wallach's representatives over the stage actor's salary. Wallach wanted $20,000 for the eight-week stint.

Because of Sinatra's interest in the role, Cohn began giving lectures on economics to Wallach's reps, pointing out that whoever played the role of Maggio was going to get an Academy Award, and so on. And that was the way the dickering continued for some time. Cohn wanted Wallach. Wallach wanted $20,000, $4,000 over what had been allotted. Sinatra would play the part for $8,000—$8,000 under the allotment.

Now Cohn huddled with his producer and director. Buddy Adler, later head of Twentieth Century–Fox, couldn't believe it when Cohn mentioned Sinatra for the Maggio part. Fred Zinnemann's eyes bulged. Daniel Taradash realized that Sinatra's gaunt appearance and streetwise, knowing manner matched the role. But . . .

According to one version of the story, Harry Cohn suddenly decided on Sinatra for the role, but couldn't persuade his staff to go along with him.

"Have you ever seen this little guy without a shirt on?" Cohn would yell at them dramatically. "This thin little guy has plenty of heart! When you see him up against Fatso, you're going to see an actor!" (Fatso is Maggio's nemesis, the sadist in charge of the stockade who eventually manages to kill Maggio.)

Meanwhile, not hearing anything from Columbia, Sinatra grew despondent. He avoided the scorching African sun and sat around in his steamy tent. When he was outside, he looked pale and drawn. He was simply sweating out the call for the screen test. At that point he had a terrible premonition that he wouldn't even get to make the test.

Frank and Ava had their marital problems, but Ava loved him and knew he was a talented and very special person—in spite of what his detractors said and in spite of his own extreme mood swings.

Privately she telephoned Cohn in Hollywood. "You've got to give that part to Frank!" she lectured Cohn.

"Ava! I've got problems with my people!"

"If he doesn't get it," Ava went on, "he'll kill himself."

Oh well, thought Cohn. What the hell?

Shortly after Ava's intervention, Cohn's office sent out a letter to Africa requesting that Sinatra make himself immediately available for a screen test at Columbia Pictures. With money borrowed from Ava, Frank flew excitedly to the Coast.

On the way he studied the book again. He was completely in tune with Maggio by now. He knew exactly what to do when he got in front of the cameras.

"For the test," Sinatra said later, "I played the saloon scene where Maggio shakes dice with the olives and the scene where he's found drunk outside the Royal Hawaiian Hotel. I was scared to death."

Buddy Adler had given him the script of the drunk scene, but Sinatra handed it back to him with the words, "I don't need this. I've read it many times."

Fred Zinnemann made the test and was so surprised and delighted that he telephoned Adler in his office. "You'd better come down here. You'll see something unbelievable. I already have it in the camera. I'm not using film this time. I want you to see it." Zinnemann had seen it, and thought to himself, If he's like that in the movie, it's a sure Academy Award.

Adler and Zinnemann had to have Harry Cohn's okay on casting, and Cohn was out of town. So they played it cool and stalled Sinatra. Frank had to leave, not knowing how much he had impressed the two men. "The next day," he said, "I flew back to Africa, probably the longest route an actor ever traveled for a fifteen-minute screen test."

But what a test! In his estimation, it was perfect. He *knew* it was good.

In Nairobi he sat around, lower than he had been before. No word came. Christ, what was the matter with those Hollywood pricks? Why didn't they call him?

Meanwhile, another act in the drama was being played out in a different part of the entertainment forest. On Broadway Elia Kazan had been working with Tennessee Williams on a new play, *Camino Real.* The script was now complete, and Kazan had been waiting for a theater vacancy to mount the production. Suddenly, toward the end of 1952, it was learned that a theater would soon be available, so the play was scheduled to go on in March 1953. Kazan began rounding up his actors. Eli Wallach had already promised Kazan he would be available to play a part in the play. Now, Wallach realized that this Broadway engagement would conflict with *From Here to Eternity*.

It put Wallach in a squeeze. He wanted the role of Maggio; he knew its worth. He also knew that Cohn was trying to get him down to $16,000. In the end, his devotion to Kazan won out. He declined the role and joined the cast of the Williams play.

Meanwhile, back in Africa, Ava was getting more and more worried about Frank. She made another clandestine telephone call to Cohn. "Give him the part, Harry!" she pleaded.

And lo and behold!

Frank Sinatra was sitting in the camp alone the next morning. A runner brought in a wire with the mail from the nearest outpost. The wire told him that he had been chosen to play the role of Maggio for the agreed-upon $8,000.

He wanted to tell somebody the good news, but there was no one around who spoke English. The actors were all out on the set. "I thought I'd go off my rocker!" he said later. Instead he went out into the jungle nearby and began shouting at the top of his voice: "I'll show those wise guys!" he yelled. "I'll show those mothers!"

He was slated to start work in March, first in Hollywood and then in Hawaii. And now, suddenly, he had a couple of nightclub commitments to fulfill before filming began. He flew out of Africa and, as a consolation present to Ava, air-freighted crates of food to her in Nairobi—mostly frozen steaks and other goodies she couldn't get in the jungle commissary. He also sent her a record player and a stack of Frank Sinatra records.

Cohn demanded that *From Here to Eternity* be brought in for $2 million, tops. He had worked closely with Adler, Zinnemann, and Taradash to hone and polish the script. He forced them to work long hours, and the story goes that one evening he even offered to take them to dinner at an expensive L.A. restaurant after work—something that was not usually in the Cohn canon of good works.

"I have no tie!" Zinnemann protested.

Cohn magnanimously buzzed the wardrobe department and said, "Bring me up three ties for Mr. Zinnemann to choose from."

The four had dinner at Perino's and returned to continue work on the script. When the session was over, Zinnemann started for the door.

"Hold it!" Cohn called. "Give me back the tie."

The Frank Sinatra who returned to Hollywood to play Maggio was not the finger-snapping nightclub artist who made singing look so easy. He knew that he had to do this role right, or it was the end of the line for him. He'd always be a has-been if this thing didn't work right for him.

And the company he was suddenly keeping was overwhelming. Burt Lancaster, an ex-circus performer, had become one of the major talents in the film business. Deborah Kerr was a top-flight star and had been for many years. And Montgomery Clift was a gifted, sensitive actor who did everything right whenever he was on camera. From the beginning, Sinatra and Clift hit it off. Instinctively, Sinatra knew that Clift was a consummate actor, and Clift sensed in Sinatra a kindred spirit. He helped Sinatra rid himself of some unnecessary mannerisms he had picked up in his song-and-dance work.

In the first two weeks of shooting in Hollywood, Sinatra tended to hide out and clutch his script in his hand, meticulously working out every nuance and every word in each scene before allowing himself to perform on the set. He was far from the relaxed singing star who had appeared in a series of lightweight musical films.

But once shooting had begun, Sinatra's obsession with perfection stood him in very good stead. His associates in the movie business had always known him as a smiling entertainer. But now, with Clift's help, he was able to assume at will the innate shrewdness and grinning insolence of the streetwise Maggio— and he knew he was making a tremendous impact on everyone who played a scene with him.

And as he worked from one setup to another, his self-confidence, never lost but definitely battered during his recent streak of lousy luck, returned in a flood. He knew he had been right about getting this part. He was on a roll.

Buddy Adler knew Cohn was serious about keeping within the $2 million budget, and he worked out a deal whereby he could ship the entire company to Hawaii by charter plane in order to save money during the three weeks allocated to outdoor location shots.

"The hell with the sight-seeing," Cohn told Zinnemann before they left. The cast arrived, exhausted and bleary-eyed, at five in the morning. And so it was that Zinnemann startled the entire group by ordering a midmorning setup *the very first day*!

Christ! thought Sinatra. It was five A.M.! No time to be up and around. Particularly with the hangovers he and half the cast had. But the actors were all professionals of the highest rank and began work as ordered. And they worked long hours from that moment on.

It was in Honolulu that Sinatra and Clift began to live it up after hours. Sinatra would always start his telephone call to Ava in Nairobi at about ten o'clock at night, and Clift would be there in his room to share a bottle. Telephoning halfway around the world was a primitive venture then, and it sometimes took Sinatra an hour to solve the network of connections. And by the time he got through, he would find that Ava was at work on the set—it was daytime in Africa, of course.

Then Sinatra and Clift would have a drink to make up for the failure to connect with Ava. Half sloshed already, the two actors would go to downtown Honolulu for a good time. They took to drinking almost competitively—scandalous behavior to the more mature and stable actors working with them.

Cohn had gone over the script line by line, and had instructed Zinnemann about the shooting of every scene. He had come to Honolulu to supervise production, and this created tension among the performers; it was well known what a problem Harry the Horror could be dealing with actors. It was in the filming of a key drunk scene between Montgomery Clift and Frank Sinatra in front of the officers' barracks at Fort De Russy that the terrible hand of Cohn came down on the actors—particularly on Sinatra, who had hoped they might all be free of his interference.

Cohn wanted the two actors to play the drunk scene standing up. But after rehearsing it standing up, Sinatra felt he could do it more naturally sitting down. By now Sinatra was almost his old self again—never taking no for an answer. Fred Zinnemann didn't particularly like the idea Sinatra had; Clift went along with the script and kept silent. It suddenly became more than a creative difference.

Sinatra objected loudly and persistently about the way the scene was being shot. When he turned to Clift for support, he got nothing more than silence. Sinatra slapped Clift on the face. But they were by now good buddies, and Clift accepted it as a typical "friendly" jab.

Zinnemann stepped in and agreed to try the scene Sinatra's way. Buddy Adler had been alerted to the confrontation and telephoned Harry Cohn at the Royal Hawaiian Hotel where he was partying with the top general of the Pacific air force.

Just as the scene was going before the cameras Sinatra's way, the cast was surprised to hear a siren pierce the air. An air-force limousine swung into view and screeched to a stop right in front of the cameras.

Cohn jumped out, fuming. Beside him was a huge general. Both men were dressed in white dinner jackets. They strode toward Zinnemann. Cohn wanted to know why the scene was being shot *wrong*.

Zinnemann outlined the situation, and Cohn grew livid.

"You let an *actor* tell you what to do?"

With some embarrassment, Zinnemann nodded.

"Why aren't you following the script?" Cohn cried.

The director was unable to come up with a satisfactory answer. While he fought for words, Cohn's face changed color. "You shoot it the way I tell you, or I am going to shut down the picture!"

Zinnemann stared at Cohn, and then at the groups of officers and air-force personnel who were standing around watching in fascination. He realized that Cohn was playing Harry the Horror. Unfortunately, Cohn had given a direct order and by doing so had painted himself into a corner. There was no way that Zinnemann could get him to change that order without making Cohn lose face. It was an impossible situation.

After a long moment of frustrated silence, Zinnemann agreed. Cohn and the general sped off in the limo, Cohn smiling and preening himself, leaving the actors to do the scene *his* way.

Sinatra was smoldering with rage. He yelled at Zinnemann and called him every name in the book for backing down in front of Cohn. Zinnemann was unresponsive. He knew where the power lay.

The scene went Cohn's way.

Zinnemann and Sinatra never did make up.

By this time Cohn knew he had a good picture— probably the greatest one he had ever produced— but he wasn't telling anyone about it. Soon, however, his pride in it became evident when the advertisements for the picture included Cohn's name along with the title of the picture. It was the first time he had ever allowed this. That meant it *had* to be good.

From Here to Eternity turned out to be the biggest moneymaker in the history of the studio. It was brought in—prints and advertising included— for the amazingly small sum of $2,406,000. In its first release, the picture grosed $19 million in theater rentals for the company! The reviewers loved it, and so did the public. The New York Film Critics gave awards to the picture, to Lancaster, and to Zinnemann. All five leading players were nominated for Academy Awards

Meanwhile, Sinatra was floundering in his private life. Ava was in Europe making another film.

She was moving around on her own. When she flew back to the States, she did not even look up her husband. Yet his work in the picture had given him new confidence and self-assurance. A week before the Academy Awards, he ate dinner in New York with song writer Jimmy Van Heusen, Sinatra's manager, Hank Sanicola, and music publisher Jackie Gale. When he and Van Heusen left for the airport to fly to Los Angeles, everybody yelled out: "Bring back that Oscar, Frank!"

"I'm getting it!" Sinatra yelled back.

Actually, he felt his chances were not that great. He was up against tough competition that year: Brandon de Wilde and Jack Palance were both nominated for *Shane*; Eddie Albert was up for his role in *Roman Holiday;* and Robert Strauss was up for *Stalag 17*.

The Awards were held that year at the Pantages Theater at Hollywood and Vine. There was a stir in the crowd of onlookers when Sinatra arrived with his teenage daughter, Nancy, and his son Frank, Jr. Where was Ava? they wondered.

Of course, to anyone with a grain of sense, it was written in the stars that Frank Sinatra would win the Academy Award. Not only was he a known personality with talent; he was also a man whose own demons had doomed him to fall from the peak of popularity. Now, the dramatic way he had engineered his own comeback by playing the role of Maggio for peanuts, made him the perfect hero of any Hollywood saga. He was the prototypical underdog who made good— not once, but twice!

. The comeback kid.

In his own words, Sinatra recalls that important and crucial night. "The minute my name was called I turned around to look at the kids. Little Nancy had tears in her eyes. For a second I didn't know whether to go up on the stage to get the Oscar or stay there and comfort her. But I gave her a peck on the cheek and reached for young Frank's hand."

He ran up to the stage and took the Oscar from the hands of a smiling Mercedes McCambridge, hugged it, looked at it, and cuddled it to his chest. Then he gave his routine thanks to Cohn, to Adler, and to Zinnemann.

As he did so, he was fighting back tears. He knew that it was the greatest thing that had ever happened to him.

He was thirty-eight years old.

He had been there before. He had been at the top. And he had fallen to the bottom.

And now he was back on the top again!

He was the hero of the quintessential American story—the triumph of the underdog.

"God chose to smile on me," he said of the Academy Award later. "It's quite a dream. I still have it three nights a week. I'd have it seven nights a week, but I don't go to bed four nights. Talk about being born again, it was one time in my life when I had such happiness I couldn't share it with another human being.

"I ducked the party, lost the crowds, and took a walk. Just me and Oscar! I think I relived my entire lifetime that night as I walked up and down the streets of Beverly Hills. Even when a cop stopped me, he couldn't bring me down to earth. It was very nice of him, although I did have to wait until his partner came cruising to assure him that I was who I said I was and that I had not stolen the statue I was carrying."

The resurrection had occurred. The myth was now on its way to being born.

★ 2 ★

Young Francis Albert

Francis Albert Sinatra was born in Hoboken, New Jersey, on December 12, 1915, the son of Anthony Martin Sinatra and Natalie Sinatra, both Italian immigrants.

Martin Sinatra, who came from Catania, a province in Sicily, was a professional prizefighter, bantamweight division. In his youth, he fought in Jersey under the name of Marty O'Brien. It was fashionable to be Irish in those days, and his blue eyes often caused him to be mistaken for Irish. At the time of his son's birth he was working as a boilermaker, engaged in war work at one of the Hoboken shipyards. It was at the beginning of World War I. Eventually he quit the shipyards to become a captain in the Hoboken Fire Department, largely through the political machinations of his wife, Natalie.

Never known by any other name except Dolly, Natalie came from Genoa, and was at the time of her son's birth a housewife of twenty. At times she would go out on jobs as a practical nurse; she was, like her mother before her, a professional midwife. Later on this strawberry-blond extrovert—she too was blue-eyed—became a force in the Democratic party in New Jersey, and at one time held the post of district leader.

Just a few blocks from the Hoboken docks, Francis Albert was delivered into this world by a doctor using old-fashioned forceps, working under extremely cramped conditions. He was a huge baby—thirteen and a half pounds! And, in fact, he was stillborn.

Dolly Sinatra's mother, Mrs. Rose Garavente, knew almost everything there was to know about childbirth. She grabbed her nonbreathing grandchild and shook him vigorously, then carried him over to a nearby water faucet and ran ice-cold water over him for a few moments until he reacted—violently. He caught his breath, gave out a lusty yell, and began breathing and screaming simultaneously. And so Frank Sinatra began life in the same manner as he lived much of it later—angry at the world, yelling, and fighting mad all the way.

Sinatra frequently bragged in his later days about his early life in the slums of Hoboken. He said, "We kids had nobody to turn to but each other. All I knew was tough kids on street corners, gang fights, and parents who were too busy trying to make enough money for food, rent, and clothes. We found a release for our loneliness and poverty in vicious gang wars. We started hooking candy from the corner store, then little things from the five-and-dime, then change from cash registers. Finally we were up to stealing bicycles."

Thus he was streetwise and independent from the beginning. These were to be keys to his character and attitude as a grown man.

It eventually became obvious that Francis Albert Sinatra would be an only child, in those days a definite no-no, particularly among the psychological fraternity. The word was that only children suffered from egotism, overprotection, domination, and overpermissiveness. Army psychologists often wrote off only children who applied for officers' training because of the persistent belief that they would crack up under pressure.

Francis Albert's aunts had a different idea about their favorite nephew. "God loved you," they told him. "He saved you for something. You're meant to *be* somebody."

From the beginning he suffered from the torments of loneliness—and rose above them. In fact, he was always popular with his peers. For one thing, he loved to dress sharply. He always appeared well accoutered, was an obsessional hand-washer, was meticulous about appearing dapper and fastidious at all times. As he grew up, he lost his baby plumpness and became skinny and even hollow-cheeked in his teen years.

Although he was bright, he seemed to focus his obvious mental acumen on subjects other than school. He went through the Hoboken public school system without making an appreciable dent in it. In fact, he annoyed his teachers at David E. Rue Junior High by doing imitations of popular movie stars and radio comics. From the beginning he was fascinated by show business and all it stood for. And he also knew how to achieve popularity with the other kids. Although small of stature, he was a good athlete. In high school he even played baseball for a while, and basketball. That was in the period before the giants stole the game from the rest of us.

Not only his father but his uncle—Lawrence Garavente, his grandmother's brother—was also a prizefighter, a welterweight. And Francis Albert always kept himself trim. He needed to. As one of the few only children in a large neighborhood of Catholic families, he was an obvious exception. He had to prove himself again and again in the streets; he had no brothers or sisters to stick up for him.

The Depression was just then beginning, and the tough guys of the movies quickly became role models for the youths on the waterfront near the Sinatra house. Frank could see these prototypes of machismo on the docks as well as in pictures. He determined to shape his own self-image into that of a dapper, sharp dresser—*and* a tough guy who could handle himself no matter who was out to get him. Sinatra created his self-image early, and was even nicknamed Slacksy O'Brien as a teenager. The O'Brien came from his father's pseudonym as a fighter, and the Slacksy referred to his sartorial bent.

About this time, he discovered singing, and learned how to strum a ukelele. Singing was a way to attract teenage girls at school; at least, that was the way a guy did it in the movies. He was successful at this—as successful as he was in taking care of himself in the streets. "I'm convinced I might have ended up in a life of crime if it hadn't been for my interest in music," Sinatra said later.

By the time he had enrolled in Demarest High School in Hoboken, he knew that he had had it with the educational system. What was it doing for him, anyway? Besides, he spent all his extra time going to see Rudy Vallee and Bing Crosby perform. But both of Frank's parents hated the idea of him being a singer. It was a great shock to Dolly when her son who could do no wrong informed her what he wanted to do with his life. She found pictures of Bing Crosby on his bedroom walls one week, and was so angry with him that she threw a shoe at him. "Why don't you want to be something *nice*—like a doctor or an engineer?" she asked.

Dolly wasn't alone in her desire for respectability and solidity. His father kept telling him, "Get something steady!"

"In your teens," Sinatra said later, "there's always someone to spit on your dreams." "Someone" was obviously his mother and his father.

It was typical of Sinatra not to hear them.

Even though the country was now sinking into the depths of the Great Depression, he managed to con his parents into purchasing a secondhand car for him. He drove it around showing off for the girls, and looking for roadhouses where he could sing to the patrons for tips.

About this time he became totally disenchanted with high school and dropped out completely. Using his car, he got an eleven-dollar-a-week job with the *Jersey Observer,* the local afternoon paper. He never did anything there but drive around and toss papers on customers' porches.

Later the story got out that he had become a very "promising sportswriter" for the paper. An "official" biography, put out by his publicist, stated that he "walked into the city room one day and gave his notice to the bewildered editor."

All baloney, of course.

A photograph of him at a typewriter, holding up a stream of teletype copy surfaces constantly, even today, with a caption reading something like this: "Here at the desk of the *Jersey Observer,* Frank pounded out sports copy and read teletype dispatches."

Dolly was impressed with her son's ability to

hang on to that eleven-dollar delivery job, and in 1932 she broke down and bought him a portable sound system that he could carry around to the nightclubs and roadhouses. He loved singing into a mike—just like the crooners of the time. In turn, he made friends with the countermen at music stores in New York City, getting free sheet music at times, which enabled him to learn the words to the songs he wanted to sing. He never did bother to learn to read music; he simply *heard* a melody and then sang it accurately and flawlessly.

It was during this time that he began taking out a young girl named Nancy Carol Barbato, the daughter of a Hoboken plasterer. He had met her at one of the big Italian family gatherings he frequented. Nancy had been hired as a secretary after learning how to type and take shorthand in high school. She liked to run around with Frank as he tried to get jobs singing in Newark, Jersey City, and even in New York.

One day in 1933 Frank took Nancy to a Jersey City theater to hear Bing Crosby. Crosby had just come from a twenty-week appearance at the Paramount Theater in New York. Bing was Frank's idol; he wanted to be another Bing.

It certainly didn't happen right away. But his so-called break came in 1935—two years later. By now his father and mother were operating a saloon at Fourth and Jefferson Streets, where a singing trio about his own age used to hang out. They called themselves the Three Flashes: Jimmy Petrozelli, Patty Principe, and Fred Tamburro. Like Frank, each thought he or she was every bit as good as Rudy Valley or Bing Crosby.

At the time one of the most popular shows was

"The Major Bowes Amateur Hour," which was staged in New York at the Capitol Theater and was broadcast on NBC radio. Bowes gave amateur performers a chance to compete with one another and provided the winners the chance to tour the country and earn seventy-five dollars a week while performing on the road.

The Three Flashes auditioned one day and were accepted. Shortly afterward, Frank Sinatra also auditioned. He too was accepted. The fact that the four young singers were from Hoboken was not lost on Bowes.

He mentioned the Three Flashes to Sinatra. "They're going to be on the show a week from Sunday. Why don't we put you on together and call you the Hoboken Four?"

The trio plus one won the contest on the night they appeared, singing a long-forgotten pop song called "Shine." They won it by the biggest vote in the history of the amateur hour—40,000 votes against a previous high of 31,000!

And the Hoboken Four went on the road as part of Major Bowes's touring company.

"We bought our own food and paid for our rooms," Sinatra recalled. Nevertheless, he began to tire of the road when they were out on the West Coast. He and the three members of the group were never really very close. "That was the first time I had ever been away. I just wanted to go home. I missed my family." And he missed the dynamism of New York just across the Hudson River.

He dropped out and came home.

By now, of course, Dolly had decided to help her son, even if she hadn't originally pictured him as a great pop singer. The music scene in the 1930s was dominated by Tin Pan Alley—actually Twenty-eighth Street in Manhattan—where most of the popular-music publishers were located. From Tin Pan Alley came the popular songs of the day, ground out by nameless men with a knack for tunes and rhymes.

Frank was finding his way around Tin Pan Alley, hustling arrangements from some of the publishers in one way or another. His second home was Fifty-second Street, where the most famous of the night-clubs were located. He haunted these places, listening to all the great singers, picking up their tricks if he could, and latching on to anything that helped make his own voice more melodious and agreeable. He was actually a light baritone, not a tenor, but he was always listed as a tenor. His type of singing was not "crooning" at all, as practiced by Bing Crosby or, earlier, Rudy Vallee, but was what is known in opera as *bel canto*—"beautiful song."

Not that Sinatra was ever a belter like Al Jolson, or, later, Frankie Laine. In the nineteenth century, tenors in opera had begun booming out their high notes from the chest, instead of floating them out with a mix of falsetto and attenuated "head tone" as they had in the earlier years of opera. In America most people were familiar with the belting-type of opera singing, not the earlier, and more classic, flexible flow of musical declaration with the melodic line subtly and sinuously supporting the poetic text of the opera libretto. Thus *bel canto* was "pure" singing as opposed to the chesty, louder, more glass-shattering singing considered "operatic" by the public.

By the time Sinatra came along, the microphone had become a necessity for the recording of music—

later to be made into "wax," actually acetate, records. Francis Albert discovered very quickly that the mike was an instrument for amplifying that sweet purity of tone he loved—the old-fashioned *bel canto* type of melody. He felt that radio technology had made possible a brand-new kind of *bel canto* for popular songs.

From the time Dolly purchased him his amplification system, he continued to work at and perfect his style. And his tone. What Sinatra wanted then was a job at a roadhouse or nightclub that was "wired"—meaning hooked up with a radio outlet that broadcast the music every night.

It was Dolly who eventually found the spot—a small place on Route 9W in Alpine, New Jersey, called the Rustic Cabin. The show there featured three comedians, along with music and singing. The music was secondary; comedy was king at the Rustic Cabin. Sinatra was hired mostly to introduce the comedians, but to do a little singing on the side.

This showcase gave him a perfect outlet five nights a week for radio exposure. He knew instinctively that radio was going to be the making of him.

He stayed at the Rustic Cabin—making the princely sum of fifteen dollars a week—for a year and a half. Just before he left, his salary was raised to twenty-five dollars a week. In those days, for an unknown singer, that was a fair wage.

During this time Sinatra began taking the only formal instruction in singing he ever had. His teacher specialized in voice exercises that would strengthen the muscles of his throat.

Sinatra never stood still with anything he had hold of. It was all well and good to operate from the

Rustic Cabin and go out on the airwaves at night, but the station was a local one and not very powerful. He began a barrage of interviews with radio-station program directors in New York City. What he wanted to do was not sing remote from somewhere outside the station, but from the studio directly. It would be a new thing.

He wasn't able to manage anything for some time.

On the personal side, a great deal was happening to him. On February 4, 1939, Sinatra celebrated his ten-dollar raise to twenty-five a week by getting married. The bride was his old girlfriend Nancy Barbato. They were married at Our Lady of Sorrows Church in Jersey City, with both families attending in the appropriate large numbers. Afterward there was a wedding reception at the Barbato home.

The ambitious singer loved Nancy, of course, but he wanted her to understand fully that he was a career man and meant to go places in the future. "I don't want anyone dragging on my neck," he told her in a gracious and friendly—but strictly Sinatra—way.

"I won't get in your way, Frank," she promised him.

Well, she didn't . . . and she did.

In a Chrysler given by the Sinatras to their son and his new bride, the newlyweds took a four-day drive to North Carolina. After their honeymoon they settled down in a third-floor walk-up in Jersey City. As a new wife, Nancy took on a job as a stenographer-typist. While she worked to help support them, Frank continued singing at the Rustic Cabin and also making his familiar moves in the music business. He parlayed his radio expertise and his knowledge of Tin Pan Alley, with its song plug-gers, countermen, and publicists, into a nice little ego-stroking, if unlucrative deal. At WNEW, an aggressive independent radio station on Fifth Ave-nue, Sinatra made a deal to sing songs from the station with an accompanist one or two days a week—without salary.

Soon after that, he found two other radio jobs—both gratis—and was appearing on three different stations! The idea, of course, was to plug the songs turned out by Tin Pan Alley writers, and get copies of the music free of charge. And manage to earn a little bit of money on the side from the pluggers.

Jimmy Rich, the station accompanist at WNEW, said about him: "He was a pusher, but polite."

Sinatra was now on three New York stations and on the Jersey airwaves as well. It was about time for *something* to happen. . . .

In 1939 Benny Goodman was the undisputed King of Swing. His great breakthrough at the Palladium in Hollywood was all part of the legend of swing. Now he was riding high, making personal appear-ances in dance halls and theaters, and performing in motion pictures and on network radio.

His star trumpet player, Harry James, wanted a band of his own; he soon broke away from Goodman to form an outfit he called the Music Makers. Good-man actually lent him a sum of money to get started. James was good—but not as good as Goodman. On his own, he was working hard to keep his head above water at the Paramount Theater in New York. That had become the mecca of swing bands. The huge theater had a capacity of five thousand.

Fretting over his lack of success in launching his

new band, James was just dropping off to sleep one night when he tuned in to WNEW's "Dance Parade," and heard a voice that struck him as melodic and sweet. At the time he was looking for singers to front for the band—singles, groups, male or female.

He telephoned the club to find out the singer's name. He was told that the club didn't *have* any singer. They had some comedians, and an emcee who "sang a little." The next night Harry James visited the Rustic Cabin. His presence caused quite a stir. Sinatra heard about it, but didn't believe it was James at all. "He wouldn't be caught dead in this joint," he declared airily.

But it *was* Harry James. He shook hands with Sinatra and told him that he could use another singer—in fact, he could use Sinatra.

"I don't have much money," James admitted.

Sinatra asked him how much he could pay.

"Seventy-five dollars a week."

That was three times what he was making at the Rustic Cabin, but he never let on to James. He reluctantly agreed to join him for the "low" seventy-five.

James liked Sinatra's combination of aggressive behavior, brash egotism, *and* humility. He said about him later: "His name is Sinatra, and he considers himself the greatest vocalist in the business. Get that! No one's ever heard of him. He's never had a hit record. He looks like a wet rag. But he says he's the greatest!"

Sinatra's first concert appearance came in June 1939, and he was reviewed in *Metronome* by George T. Simon, who spoke of the "very pleasing vocals of Frank Sinatra, whose easy phrasing is especially commendable."

It was at this time that James and Sinatra recorded an undistinguished tune titled "All or Nothing at All," which some song plugger had persuaded them to do. The record began selling a little, and by the end of the year had reached the unimpressive total of about 8,000 sales. That song, of course, later . . .

The James band had a woman singer from Georgia named Marie Antoinette Yvonne Jamais. James didn't like her name; it sounded just like his—except for the Marie Antoinette part, of course. So he made her change it. She became Connie Haines.

When the band went on the road, radio began to do exactly what Sinatra had predicted it would do for him. It was making him known to the public.

Even Connie Haines was impressed. "The first theater we played on the road with James was the Hippodrome in Baltimore," she recalled. "The kids were hanging around the stage door, screaming for Frank. Later people said that those kids were 'plants.' Plants! That's ridiculous. Who could afford plants? James? He was always broke!"

When they got to California, Frank Sinatra was hoping for some break in the movies, but James's music was loud and brassy—too much for the people at Victor Hugo's in Hollywood where they were booked. "The owner kept telling us we were playing too loud," James said. "And so he wouldn't pay us. We were strugglng pretty good and nobody had any money, so Frank would invite us up to his [low-rent] place and Nancy would cook spaghetti for everyone."

Indeed the band was in trouble. It was heading for a breakup. Sinatra was no fool. He sensed the end was coming and continued to search for other work. Although an end of sorts came for the James organization right there in Hollywood, James started up again in Chicago at the Sherman Hotel. By then, however, it was time for Frank to get his break.

Early in 1940 a song plugger who was trying to peddle a song to Tommy Dorsey observed the way the bandleader listened to a record that had been cut by James and Sinatra in 1939—"All or Nothing at All." The song plugger, who had brought it to Dorsey—in order to plug the song, not the singer—recalled the scene: "Tommy just sits there taking in this vocal. It seems to intrigue him. He likes this guy Sinatra."

It was less that Dorsey "liked this guy Sinatra" than that he was getting annoyed at his steady singer, Jack Leonard, who was threatening to leave him and go out on his own. To teach Leonard a lesson, Dorsey wanted to bring in someone else as a threat to his star.

In Chicago Sinatra learned through the grapevine that Dorsey was having troubles with Leonard. Dorsey, appearing at the Palmer Hotel in Chicago at the time, knew the James band had broken up and was in the first stages of repair right down the street at the Sherman Hotel. Sinatra and Dorsey finally met. Each was playing the same game: Dorsey the reluctant buyer, Sinatra the reluctant goods.

Dorsey listened to Sinatra. He was visibly impressed, but made no promises—"We'll call you," or words to that effect. Sinatra went back to James, waiting for the call. Then, through the same grapevine, Dorsey let Sinatra know that he was going to hire another singer. Sinatra fell for it and called another meeting. This time they took off the masks and settled on a fee. It was $100 a week. Cheap for Dorsey. But more than Sinatra was getting from James.

James was magnanimous. He knew that Nancy Sinatra was pregnant at the time; he knew Frank needed the extra money. He told Frank to go to Dorsey—with his blessings.

Sinatra was to join the band two weeks later in Milwaukee. Jack Egan, a veteran press agent, was handling Dorsey then. He recalled that Sinatra didn't sing at all in Milwaukee, during a theater engagement. Through some odd turn of events, Sinatra had no arranger, and when he made his first appearance with the band at the Lyric Theater in Indianapolis, he had only two songs he could sing. The first was a ballad, "My Prayer," and the second was "Marie," which was Dorsey's big-band number, and Jack Leonard's smash hit.

Egan said: "Well, [Sinatra] broke it up completely" —the crowd, that is. "And that was tough to do because a lot of the kids were big Jack Leonard fans. They kept yelling for more, but Frank had no encore prepared. So there right onstage he and Tommy went into a huddle and Frank suggested they fake 'South of the Border.'

"Well, that broke it up even more, especially when Frank started slurring down on those notes. You know, right then and there, when he went into the slurring bit, the kids started screaming, just the way they did later at the Paramount. And there was nothing rigged about it, either. I know, because I was the band's press agent. And I was also Jack

35

Leonard's close friend, and I wasn't inclined to go all out for any other singer. No, those screams were real!"

The Dorsey band was on a roll now. Sinatra blossomed with Dorsey, and the Dorsey band bloomed with Sinatra. Dick Jones, a Dorsey arranger and later a close friend of Sinatra, said simply, "Frank's musical taste was developed at Tommy's elbow."

Sinatra was working hard now. He could feel how he aroused the patrons when he sang. He now knew he was as good as he had suspected he was. What he needed was work, work, work. And he was tireless about getting it.

Jo Stafford, a member of the Pied Pipers, recalled Frank and his ability to "woodshed" everything for the proper effect. After Frank had joined the Dorsey band, he tried to blend his voice with the backup of the Pied Pipers. A quartet at the time, the Pipers included Jo Stafford, Chuck Lowrey, Clark Yocum, and John Huddleston. (Actually, the Pipers had started out as an octet—eight singers, male and female—but Dorsey kept losing singers and couldn't afford to hire on any replacements!) "Most solo singers usually don't fit too well into a group," Stafford admitted, "but Frank never stopped working at it and, of course, as you know, he blended beautifully with us. He was meticulous about his phrasing and dynamics. He worked very hard so that his vibrato would match ours. And he was always conscientious about learning his parts."

In the meantime, while he was on the road, Frank Sinatra's first child, a girl named Nancy, was born in June 8, 1940.

In spite of all the hard work and in spite of his own instinct that he was very good, fame eluded

Sinatra. He was still nowhere. The reviews didn't make him too happy. *Billboard* magazine said he was a good ballad singer, "but nil on showmanship." Looked at in later years, that comment can go down as the most "clouded crystal ball" statement of the era.

Sinatra came in twenty-second in the *Billboard* Collegiate Choice of Male Vocalists, with Jack Leonard in the Number Two spot. Dorsey was upset that Ray Eberle of the Glenn Miller band was Number One, and Bob Eberle (Ray's brother) of Tommy's brother Jimmy's band was Number Three. "I got to have a record!" Sinatra began saying to himself.

Dorsey was running a contest for new song writers. A woman named Ruth Lowe, who was playing piano in a Toronto sheet-music shop, was trying to break into the song-writing business. Just after her husband died during an operation, she wrote a song called simply, "I'll Never Smile Again." Connie Haines remembered the contest. "Tommy couldn't be bothered going through all that mail, so he made Frank and me do it. It was a grab bag. You couldn't look at all of it. Besides, neither Frank nor I could read music."

They picked the Lowe song. Something about it seemed fresh and real. "I got ten dollars for recording it," Haines said. "Frank got twenty-five."

The song became a major hit.

Finally Frank Sinatra's growing popularity began to be reflected in the various fan magazines: he hit the Number One spot in *Billboard*'s annual College Music Survey in May 1941, and then was selected as Number One in the *Down Beat* poll and as best male band singer of the year by *Metronome,* both in January 1942. Now he really had arrived.

★ 3 ★

The Voice

It was a silken smoothness of melody that Sinatra was after—a satiny, sweet, and honeylike quality. And to sing that way, he had to phrase his melodic line so he could sing for a long time without pausing to take a breath. Although he had learned quite a bit about holding a long note from his one encounter with a voice instructor, a great deal of his mellow, endlessly flowing tone had come from constant observation and study of other singers, plus practice, practice, practice.

Now, while on the road with the Dorsey band, he began to see how the trombonist—Dorsey himself—was able to sustain a note without making any apparent breath. *Apparent* was the operative word.

"I used to sit behind him on the bandstand and watch, trying to see him sneak a breath," Sinatra wrote in a *Life* magazine piece. "But I never saw the bellows move in his back. His jacket didn't even move. I used to edge my chair to the side a little, and peek around to watch him."

And then Sinatra learned the trick.

"I discovered that he had a 'sneak' pinhole in the corner of his mouth—not an actual pinhole, but a tiny place where he was breathing. In the middle of a phrase, while the tone was still being carried through the trombone, he'd go shhhh and take a quick breath and play another four bars with that breath."

Why couldn't a singer do that? Sinatra wondered. The answer was, of course, that a singer could.

"The first thing I needed was extraordinary breath control, which I didn't have." To achieve this, he began a regimen of swimming as often as he could. He would swim underwater, holding his breath for as long as possible. "I worked out on the track at the Stevens Institute in Hoboken," he said, "running one lap, trotting the next. Pretty soon I had good breath control, but that still wasn't the whole answer. I still had to learn to sneak a breath without being too obvious."

Practicing what he had learned from Dorsey—a technique called "circular breathing" by other professionals—Sinatra finally perfected his phrasing until he could hold a note almost six bars long, and sometimes eight, without visibly gulping in air. Six or eight was a big improvement over the usual two or four bars of most singers. Now he was inhaling through the nose and exhaling through the mouth—*at the same time*.

"This gave the melody a flowing, unbroken quality, and that—if anything—was what made me sound different," Sinatra wrote.

What Sinatra did, in effect, was to create the impression that he did not breathe at all, and that he simply sang through exuberance—or, perhaps, through divine inspiration. It was all part of the creation of a myth of perfection.

Not only did Dorsey teach him, inadvertently, how to sing without visibly taking breaths; he also gave him an insight on how to handle large groups of teenage music lovers. Sinatra, though, was developing his own strategies for dealing with his admirers. He probably understood the mythology of the fan better, by instinct, than Dorsey did himself.

One teenager, who later became a television producer, tried to get an autograph from the bandleader after a night's gig in Portland, Maine. Dorsey had him tossed out of the area in a Howard Johnson Restaurant he had reserved for band members. The teenager, Paul Keyes, followed Sinatra into the men's room, still hoping to ask for his autograph. Sinatra obliged, striking up a conversation. Keyes told him how Dorsey had had him thrown out of the restaurant.

"Come with me, kid," Sinatra said, and took Keyes into the room where the side men were eating. He introduced him to Ziggy Elman, Connie Haines, Jo Stafford, Buddy Rich, and all the other members of the orchestra. "This is my friend Paul. Write something nice to him in his autograph book."

Finally, Sinatra took Keyes over to Dorsey. "Tommy," Sinatra said with a smile, "this is my friend Paul, and I want you to write something nice in his book. He's a good kid."

Dorsey, recognizing Keyes instantly but not letting on, graciously did as Sinatra requested.

Fans. Sinatra understood the value of fans long before he really had a great number of them. But that rapport stood him in good stead in later years. Mainly, work in the Dorsey band gave him the exposure that he greatly needed.

41

During his stint with Dorsey, the band appeared in several movie sequences (one of them was *Las Vegas Nights,* made at Paramount in 1941) and also on network radio programs. He was even allowed to take bows from the stages of some of the biggest and most posh motion-picture houses in the entire country. But mostly, it was through Dorsey's records that Sinatra became recognized as a singing voice on jukeboxes all over the nation.

He had learned quite a bit on his own, of course, even before appearing with James and Dorsey. There was that personal obsession with cleanliness that he had always had, that need to be a sharp dresser. The Dorsey side men were awed from the beginning by his personal habits. "Why, he changed his shirt every day!" one of them exclaimed in disbelief. "Sometimes he took two or three baths a day, and he was always washing his hands. Also, damned if he didn't refuse to eat from a dirty plate." That seemed to be the accolade of the day.

With Dorsey's recording of "I'll Never Smile Again," the grab-bag hit, Sinatra was the undisputed main attraction of the Dorsey orchestra. People began to come out to see Sinatra, not Dorsey.

This did not sit at all well with Dorsey. After all, he was the leader of the band, and he was the one paying the salaries. Also, he was a touchy, temperamental person—he couldn't even get along with his brother Jimmy well enough to continue in partnership. News of Sinatra's growing importance was indeed *bad* news to him.

Dorsey wasn't alone in his jealousy of Sinatra. Buddy Rich was Dorsey's drummer, and when the teenagers began crowding around the bandstand to listen to Sinatra's singing, Rich began to bang out the beat so heavily that he sometimes overwhelmed Sinatra's voice with the noise.

Sinatra got so mad at him one night he tossed a pitcher filled with water and ice cubes at the drummer backstage—luckily missing him and avoiding real trouble and perhaps even a lawsuit.

The tension only got worse as Sinatra's popularity grew. It was finally Sinatra who got fed up with Dorsey. Sinatra was big stuff. Even if he wasn't featured on the labels, everybody knew who he was. When it said "Vocal Chorus" underneath Dorsey's name, the fans all knew it was Sinatra doing the singing. Frank now put the screws to Dorsey. He wanted to do solos with his own name on the label.

To Frank's surprise, Dorsey caved in pretty easily. At least, he seemed to cave in. He instructed Axel Stordahl, his arranger, to work up a number of singing solos for Frank. They were "The Night We Called It a Day" backed by "Night and Day," and "The Song Is You" backed by "Lamplighter's Serenade."

Sinatra discovered Dorsey's ploy when the records were issued: they were marketed under the Bluebird label, not Victor. Victor records cost seventy-five cents; while Bluebird records cost only thirty-five cents—the Bluebird label was a cheapie designed to sell at depressed rates. Actually, Sinatra was being gypped out of royalties. Undeterred, he recorded "There Are Such Things" in July, 1942. Although Sinatra and Dorsey didn't know it at the time, it was to be the last recording they made together.

By now Frank's salary had increased from $100 a week to $250. But even in those days he could never keep a nickel in his pocket. He was a big spender, picking up restaurant checks, buying the side men drinks in bars, and taking out groups of friends and hangers-on for nights on the town.

But ambition was gnawing at the core of Frank Sinatra. Sure, he had a great spot in the limelight with Dorsey, one of the best showcases of the era. Sure, he could go on forever. But he wondered what it would be like to be out on his own—and make it big there!

He had picked up the rudiments of financial chicanery from Dorsey. He knew Dorsey had gotten him cheap when he had hired on. He knew Dorsey had swindled him by putting his solos on Bluebird. Now he decided he wanted to be entirely on his own, so he could collect the whole gate rather than just a weekly paycheck.

Along the way, Sinatra had been looking around for people to help him get bookings when he did decide to go out on his own. He found ready representation with General Amusement Corporation, later called General Artists Corporation. He also managed to interest Columbia Records in a deal, although the head, Mannie Sachs, had to be pressured to take him on; it was the polls with Sinatra's name in conspicuous spots that finally convinced Sachs. So he switched from R.C.A. to Columbia Records.

Now came the hard part. Sinatra had signed a contract with Dorsey and Dorsey's business manager, Leonard Vannerson. When the two men looked over the contract, they found it was airtight, and refused to part with Sinatra. The contract said he had signed exclusively with them, and as far as they were concerned, it would remain in effect.

Sinatra was getting lessons in business the hard way.

But, of course, Dorsey and Vannerson thought they could work out some kind of deal. These were the numbers: in return for 43⅓ percent of Sinatra's gross income for the next ten years, Dorsey and Vannerson would agree to let him go out on his own.

How could a shrewdie like Sinatra let himself get tangled up in such a financial mess?

"He would have given *anybody* a piece of him then," a friend said later in explanation.

At that time, indeed, *Down Beat* calculated that with additional fees and taxes owed in various places, a least 93⅓ percent of Frank Sinatra's earnings were owed to someone other than Sinatra! By some calculations, the figure was said to exceed 100 percent.

Within a very short time, Sinatra realized that he had not cut a very brilliant deal with Dorsey. While he was with Dorsey, he didn't know in what direction things were heading. Once he had got out and his career began to shape up, it was a different story. So why was he paying Dorsey for not working for him?

In a newspaper story printed about six months after he had quit Dorsey, Sinatra said: "You may quote Sinatra as saying that he believes it is wrong for anybody to own a piece of him and collect on it when that owner is doing nothing for Sinatra."

The reason for the quote was that Sinatra had finally decided to refuse to pay up on the contract. When the money did not come through, Dorsey attached Sinatra's earnings. Sinatra retaliated by urging his fans to boycott the theaters where Dorsey was appearing. It was actually a fairly amusing situation—and typical of the times and of the personalities involved.

M.C.A.—the country's biggest booking agency—stepped into the breach and came up with a deal. If Sinatra moved from G.A.C. to M.C.A. for his bookings, M.C.A. would pay Vannerson and Dorsey $35,000 to get Sinatra out of the contract. In addition, Sinatra was to give M.C.A. $25,000—the money lent to him by Columbia Recording Corporation as a gesture of goodwill against his upcoming record royalties. G.A.C. and M.C.A. also agreed to split their commissions on Sinatra's earnings until 1948.

Sinatra now got back all the percentages that other people had owned. "I now own myself," he proudly told the media.

These are the facts about the buyout of the Dorsey-Vannerson contract as they are recorded in the public annals. But there is also a rumor to the effect that Frank Sinatra exerted a bit of friendly Sicilian persuasion on Dorsey and Vannerson to get his contract broken.

Although at the time little was known to the public about Sinatra's alleged association with mobsters and members of what came to be called the Mafia in later years, Sinatra had been friendly with quite a few people who had connections in one way or another with the so-called mob. And even then it was common knowledge among the cognoscenti in the entertainment business that some celebrities were sponsored by underworld figures.

Anyway, as the story goes—and it occasionally resurfaces even now, some forty years later—when Dorsey refused to accept payment for Sinatra's proposed buyout, he was visited by one Quarico Moretti (reputed to be the Mafia boss of New Jersey and also known as Willie Moretti and Willie Moore) in his dressing room one night. According to the story, Moretti pulled out a handgun and shoved the barrel in Dorsey's mouth, suggesting in a soft but persuasive voice that he sell Sinatra's contract back to him.

The sum mentioned was one dollar.

As any film buff knows, that legendary story was dramatized in the motion picture *The Godfather*.

True?

False?

Who knows?

But it adds spice to the mythology and methodology of Frank Sinatra.

His break with Dorsey was to be the end of Sinatra's day with the big bands—and from that moment on he was strictly on his own as a singer and entertainer. In spite of all the problems and drawbacks, he always remembered his big-band showcasing days with nostalgia: "Whether you were an instrumentalist or a vocalist, working in a band was an important part of growing up, musically and as a human being. It was a career builder, a seat of learning, a sort of cross-country college that taught you about collaboration, brotherhood, and sharing rough times. When it comes to professional experience, there's nothing to beat those one-nighter tours, when you rotate between five places around the clock—the bus, your hotel room, the greasy-spoon restaurant, the dressing room (if any), and the bandstand. Then back on the bus to the next night's gig, maybe four hundred miles away or more.

"I've said this many times, but it can never be

said too often: a singer can learn, should learn, by listening to musicians. My greatest teacher was not a vocal coach, not the work of other singers, but the way Tommy Dorsey breathed and phrased on the trombone."

Actually, it was not a propitious time for Frank Sinatra to break with the big-band world. In August 1942 a bitter strike broke out between the American Federation of Musicians, under the leadership of Cesar Petrillo, and the record industry. Singers, however, were not technically bound by the strike—only musicians. It was wartime, and perhaps the strike had less effect than it might have had in ordinary times. Sinatra and Columbia Records offered some rather odd a capella renditions of new songs.

Sinatra, now on his own, made his first solo appearance on December 30, 1942, at the Paramount Theater in New York as an "Extra Added Attraction" with Benny Goodman and his Orchestra.

Goodman, a very hip and polished musician and bandleader—the King of Swing—was unprepared for the chaos that erupted when Sinatra appeared on stage. In fact, when he was first informed that Sinatra was on the bill, he frowned and asked: "Who the hell is he?"

Now, with the band in place, and Sinatra suddenly appearing in full view, things began to happen.

"The sound that greeted me was absolutely deafening," Sinatra recalled later. "It was a tremendous roar. I was scared stiff. I couldn't move a muscle. Benny froze, too. He turned around, looked at the audience, and asked, 'What the hell was that?' I burst out laughing and gave out with 'For Me and My Gal.' "

Sinatra's amusement was appropriate. At the time of his Paramount appearance, he had just hired a publicist named George Evans to "build him up." He felt he needed help. Evans had worked for Glenn Miller's orchestra and for other musicians to make them more appealing to the public.

Sinatra knew that Evans had something cooking. Later Evans confessed that before his new client's appearance at the Paramount, he had assembled a gaggle of teenage girls in the basement of the Paramount Theater and had rehearsed them in yelling, squealing, and swooning when Sinatra appeared and sang. But pay them? Never!

Evans later offered $1,000, to be donated to the favorite charity of anyone who could prove that any person was given "a ticket, a pass, a gift, or a gratuity of any kind in any shape or manner at all to go in and screech." The stakes would later be raised to $5,000.

Nevertheless, upon closer questioning, Evans did admit that perhaps Sinatra's acclaim was not always entirely—well, *spontaneous*. "Certain things were done," he noted. "It would be as wrong for me to divulge them as it would be for a doctor to discuss his work." E. J. Kahn, Jr., put it a little more succinctly in his piece on Sinatra titled "The Voice" in the *New Yorker*. "Evans," the story said, "went to work on American womanhood."

Evans's ploy snowballed. With the news that Paramount patrons were squealing and swooning all over the place, teenage America began squealing and swooning from coast to coast.

With beautiful timing, Frank Sinatra made his debut on CBS network radio just a month after his spectacular appearance at the Paramount. He was the star of the most famed and listened-to show of the time, "Your Hit Parade," a Saturday-night institution that included the top ten songs of the week, plus an occasional "extra." Sinatra's first song was such a "Lucky Strike Extra": "Night and Day."

Needless to say, with the nation's teenagers lined up solidly behind him, Sinatra became all the rage on the "Hit Parade." But he needed to parlay his popularity into solo appearances. He was making it on radio, in the motion-picture theaters, and in the movies, but no one really knew whether he would draw patrons in a nightclub. After all, nightclubs were expensive.

At this time G.A.C. was still handling Frank, and his contact there was the head of the café department, Harry Kilby. It was Kilby who came up with the proper "image" for Sinatra. He nicknamed him "The Voice." Earl Wilson related the story in his book *Sinatra*.

Managers of the big joints on Fifty-second Street all sneered at Kilby when he came around peddling Sinatra. They'd never heard of the man, and certainly they thought that calling him "The Voice" was the goddamned dumbest thing they had ever heard.

The Riobamba Club, five blocks away from the bright lights and the money of Fifty-second Street, was almost out of business at the time. It was getting ready to roll over and die. Through some shenanigans with a pair of press agents he knew who were willing to help him out to save the Riobamba, Kilby conned the club into hiring Sinatra for $750 a week. Sinatra didn't like the money; he knew he was being trimmed. And there was more bad news. A comic and a singer were getting top billing over him.

Sinatra burned. He came in and looked the place over and commented to the management: "They'll have to bust the walls of this joint." The management didn't think too highly of this egotistical guy from Hoboken.

Evans mounted a promo for the "Extra Added Attraction," as Sinatra was billed—they now called him "Swoonatra" to tie him in with the Paramount swooners Evans had developed—and it was a dilly.

On March 11, 1943, Sinatra opened as the third attraction at Riobamba—he was playing second banana to Walter O'Keefe, and first banana to Sheila Barrett—and he was a solid hit from the beginning.

One woman fainted. Had one of Evans's ubiquitous assistants turned up the heat downstairs? It *was* hot in the club.

But then, so was Sinatra.

Two nights later the front door of the Riobamba resembled the front door of the Paramount Theater when Sinatra appeared there. By the end of the week, Sinatra had turned the club's fortunes around and himself into a national phenomenon.

Evans's "Swoonatra" gimmick appeared to have paid off big. Now columnists and writers in all parts of the world of entertainment were making up their own versions of it. People were calling him a "Swoonheart." Teenagers were going into "Sinatrances." Young women were afflicted with "Sinatritis." "Swoonology" became a popular course in some college curriculums. "Sinatramania" had infected the country. He was "Sinattractive." The "Sinatroops" were in charge overseas.

Dorothy Kilgallen wrote that "Sinatra'd" was a

new synonym for "mobbed." Walter Winchell came up with another meaning for "Sinatra'd": the past tense of a verb that meant "to cut up into several financial pieces," in reference to his problems with Tommy Dorsey. When Frank appeared at the Paramount in April 1943 the theater was temporarily renamed the "Parasinatra."

Ouch!

But the media members didn't stop with the name. In addition to Kilby's masterful "The Voice," columnists called Sinatra the "Lean Lark," "Moonlight Sinatra," the "Swoon Kid," the "Sultan of Swoon," "The Larynx," the "Svengali of Swing," and even his old high-school moniker, "Angles." That always came out "Angels"—but what the hell?

Not all were entranced. In an August 1943 column, Elsa Maxwell called Sinatra "actually the glorification of ignorance, musical illiteracy, and the power of fake, synthetic, raw publicity in its greatest arrogance—propaganda in its most cynical form."

Even that barb was fated to be dulled. After a meeting with Sinatra in November 1943, Maxwell wrote, "I found a simple, unspoiled singer of songs." The next summer she was completely enthralled, calling Sinatra "my bête noire," and in 1945, "my adopted son."

Poor Ben Gross, radio editor of the *New York Daily News,* who had the temerity to write that he did not consider Sinatra the greatest singer in the world. One fan wrote in suggesting that Gross "should burn in oil, pegs should be driven into your body, and you should be hung by your thumbs." Another fan told him that she would "love to take you to Africa, tie you to the ground, pour honey on you, and let the ants come and bite you to pieces."

When Columbia Records rereleased the Harry James recording of "All or Nothing at All" in May 1943, it gave top billing to Sinatra, not James. This time around the record, which had sold 8,000 copies in its first pressing, went over a million copies and placed Number Two for the year.

In the summer of 1943, Sinatra cut his first recordings for Columbia Records, with an a cappella backup because of the musicians' strike. One of the sides was "You'll Never Know," by Mack Gordon and Harry Warren, which won the Academy Award for best movie song for 1943. It originally appeared in a long-forgotten Twentieth Century–Fox movie titled *Hello, Frisco, Hello,* starring Alice Faye and John Payne.

Although Sinatra had been in several motion pictures already, he had signed no regular contract but had appeared each time on a one-shot basis as a singer. Now at last he was beginning to be noticed by Hollywood, and in the summer of 1943 RKO-Radio Pictures signed him to one of their standard contracts, to begin work in the fall of the year.

He also wangled a special booking to appear at the Hollywood Bowl—a real coup for a pop singer. The trip to the West Coast galvanized the studio flack into action, and when Sinatra traveled by railroad to Los Angeles, it was announced that an escort of twenty-five policemen would be used to protect the singer from his fans on arrival at Union Station.

This plan turned out to be a feint, however. He was actually scheduled to disembark secretly at Pasadena instead of downtown L.A. But—and this was where the flack got to work—the "secret" was leaked out deliberately . . . on radio! The studio even sent a collection of its bit players to greet him at Pasadena, covering their bet in case nobody showed up.

They need not have bothered. As the train screeched to a stop in the home of the Rose Bowl, the streets were already teeming with screaming, almost hysterical fans assembled en masse to meet the train and their hero. It was estimated that at least 5,000 celebrants were there to commemorate the event. In the chaos that resulted, one reporter was even bitten in the arm by a rabid fan.

Sinatra was to begin work on the first movie in which he would act as well as sing. But before he had a chance to settle down at the studio on Gower and Santa Monica, he had the singing engagement to fulfill.

On August 14, he appeared at the Hollywood Bowl in a solo performance that brought frowns and groans from West Coast highbrows who felt only opera and symphonic music were appropriate fare for the Bowl—but loving screams and shrieks from devoted fans.

Then he got down to work. The title of the film he was making was *Higher and Higher*, based on a Broadway musical that in turn had been based on a stage play by Josh Logan and Gladys Hurlbut. In its usual astuteness, the studio threw out all the original songs—written by the redoubtable team of Richard Rodgers and Lorenz Hart!—and assigned Harold Adamson and Jimmy McHugh to write some new numbers. Luckily, one of them, "I Couldn't Sleep a Wink Last Night," hit the big time, largely because of Sinatra's inspired rendition of it.

The plot of the movie? Sinatra is a rich young man in love with a scullery maid posing as a debutante; she marries the butler. When the picture was finally released, the headline for Bosley Crowther's *New York Times* review suggested that the title be revised from *Higher and Higher* to *Lower and Lower*.

Sinatra's contract gave him the opportunity to work in at least one film a year away from RKO: and what a break that was! The first film under that deal would be *Anchors Aweigh* for MGM—after *Step Lively* at RKO, a weak remake of the Marx Brothers big hit *Room Service*.

The rage for Sinatra continued to mount, with some psychologists suggesting that the mania was linked to the fact that most American men were away fighting in others parts of the world. That may have been part of the madness—but not all.

The ballads Sinatra sang were *aimed* at lonely women and lonely men; they were blues songs, songs of frustrated love, of sentimental attachment, of dreams of romance. The formula of the songs was perfect for the times: they celebrated the love of two people separated for the time being and achingly lonely for one another.

And, of course, the question did remain in some minds as to why, if so many other men were fighting, Sinatra was not. Once again a little backstage drama played right into the hands of Sinatra's publicists.

Late in 1943, Frank Sinatra was classified 1A by his draft board, and when his "greetings" arrived, he was instructed to report for induction on January 12, 1944.

"I'll go any time they say," Sinatra stated patriotically. "My wife is going to have another baby in a couple of months. I hope it's a boy."

He reported for his pre-induction physical at Newark, New Jersey, and underwent the same boring examination that millions of other males were undergoing. Only in the case of Francis Albert Sinatra, the doctors found that a series of mastoid operations in his early youth had resulted in a punctured eardrum.

That was enough to render him ineligible for service. He was classified 4F and sent back to the entertainment world. The *New York Post* headlined the news:

THE ARMY SWOONS—SINATRA IS 4F

And so he was back—without having gone anywhere. He continued to sing, and continued to pack in the menless women, and Evans continued to pour out his press releases, motivating those menless women to go out to see and hear The Voice.

Arriving in Boston for a personal appearance, Sinatra was met at the station by 3,000 yelling women. One, swinging her hand at him to touch him, scratched a plainclothes detective in the face with her fingernails. Another fan, frustrated by a rumor that Sinatra had been contributing all of his fan mail to a wastepaper drive, tried to tackle him in a high-dive from a divan in the hotel lobby.

In the Boston armory, the management ordered the seats bolted to the floor to prevent them from being ripped apart for souvenirs. In Chicago, a hundred excited girls smashed the windows of a train bringing Sinatra into town. A woman handing him a bouquet of flowers knocked down a bishop who had come to observe the scene. In Trenton, New

Jersey, thousands of girls heard that Sinatra was
going to make a speech at the convention of the
United Steelworkers of America; they almost tore
the place up when they found out it wasn't true.

But the Paramount Theater in New York was
still the "shrine of their disorder," in the words of
E. J. Kahn, Jr. "No holds are barred there," one
Sinatra fan said. "That's the home of swoon."

The Sinatra wave reached its peak on October 12,
1944, at Times Square's Paramount Theater in
what became known as the "Columbus Day Riot."
By that time the name Sinatra was enough to
stir anyone to action one way or another. American servicemen in the far reaches of the globe
went into fits of rage over the popularity of this
upstart who was not fighting by their sides but
instead was making out with all the women left
at home. On the other hand, the women of America—
if they were lucky enough to be near a theater
featuring him—were going out and buying special
outfits, having their hair done, and in general,
preening themselves to the utmost for the occasion.

The Paramount Theater had 3,600 seats, and was
offering six or seven showings a day of the motion
picture *Our Hearts Were Young and Gay*. But nobody came to see the movie. They came to see
Frank Sinatra.

Common practice was to allow any seated customer to stay for as many performances as desired.
During a Sinatra appearance, it became customary
for his fans to retain their seats all through the
day, and even on into the night. The patrons would
hold their seats, talking with each other all through
the movie, even "peeing in their places rather than

relinquishing their seats," as John Rockwell put it in *Sinatra: An American Classic*.

One usher described it this way: "That Sinatra hits those kids right in the kidneys."

Anyway, on Columbus Day, 1944, only 250 of the 3,500 inside left the theater after the first showing of *Our Hearts Were Young and Gay*. At the same time, there were 30,000 more fans outside, waiting to be let in! The line—about six abreast—extended west on Forty-third Street, north up Eighth Avenue, and back east on Forty-fourth Street. Cars were having a hard time getting through Times Square. Finally, after several hours, it became apparent to those outside that even if they had their tickets, they weren't going to get inside at all. Shock waves rippled through the crowd, and suddenly it became a mob and it reacted. The standees began venting their wrath on whatever was near them—smashing windows of shops, jumping out into the street and stopping cars, running wild on the sidewalks and in the streets.

Over on Fifth Avenue, the Columbus Day parade was getting started, when suddenly all the cops were summoned to Times Square, where they leaped into the fray. At the height of the melee there were 421 police reserves, twenty radio cars, two emergency trucks, four lieutenants, six sergeants, two captains, two assistant chief inspectors, two inspectors, seventy patrolmen, fifty traffic cops, twelve mounted policemen, twenty policewomen, and two hundred detectives trying to control some 30,000 wild teenage fans.

They fainted, fell down, shrieked, broke things open, assaulted the ticket booth of the theater and destroyed it, smashed more windows.

A frightened Frank Sinatra huddled inside, munching on food smuggled in from the famous Sardi's restaurant, located next door. He could hear the cries of "Frankie, Frankie!" outside, along with the occasional screams.

An amused, hardly worried George Evans was eating with him.

Sinatra was gloomy. "I'll have to stay here all day!"

"If you try to go out, you'll be killed. You'll be torn limb from limb." It was hard for Evans to hide his smile of elation.

The media were quick to the attack. Little of the "riot" was attributed to Sinatra's amazing popularity or his ability to sing. It was decided instead that he was filling a void left by absent soldiers. His punctured left eardrum was again brought up for scrutiny. Psychologists decided that the riot was due to an innate "mothering" instinct in women; they wanted to mother Sinatra because, with his bad eardrum, the poor dear was 4F.

Oh?

In a 1974 article in the *New York Times Magazine,* a bobby soxer from those days recalled what it was like to go out to see Sinatra. She had done so in Boston at the RKO-Boston Theater.

"We *loved* to swoon," she wrote. "Back from the RKO-Boston, we would gather behind locked bedroom doors, in rooms where rosebud wallpaper was plastered over with pictures of The Voice, to practice swooning. We would take off our saddle shoes, put on his records and stand around groaning for a while. Then the song would end and we would all fall down on the floor. We would do that for an hour or so."

She went on: "We were sick all right. Crazy. The sociologists were out there in force.... What yo-yo's. Whatever he stirred beneath our barely budding breasts, it wasn't motherly. And the boys knew that and that was why none of them liked him.... Frankie was *sexy*. It was exciting. It was terrific."

And: "I used to bring binoculars just to watch that lower lip [of his]. And then, the other thing: The voice had that *trick*, you know, that funny little sliding, skimming slur it would do coming off the end of a note; it drove us bonkers ... it was an invitation to hysteria. He'd give us that little slur— 'All ... or nothing at aallll ...'—and we'd start swooning all over the place."

It couldn't last forever, of course. Sinatra knew that. So did Evans.

Both of them were right. But it all came to an end—or what *seemed* to be the end—much more quickly than they had imagined.

★ 4 ★

Down and Down I Go

The Columbus Day riot of 1944 at the Paramount Theater was the peak of Frank Sinatra's professional career thus far. It was a career that had been escalating at an incredible, dizzying speed, while at home in New Jersey, the second Sinatra child, Franklin Wayne, was born on January 10, 1944. Little Nancy was three and a half then.

Every record Sinatra made was an almost sure-fire hit: "You'll Never Know," "Sunday, Monday, or Always," "I Couldn't Sleep a Wink Last Night," "Saturday Night (Is the Loneliest Night in the Week)," and "I've Got the World on a String."

And there was one other song, too—one that Sinatra made a special part of his repertoire. And the writing on that song was a story in itself.

There was a party held around a swimming pool in Hollywood one day, with the song writer Jimmy Van Heusen and his partner, Johnny Burke, who had written dozens of numbers sung by Sinatra. Burke's wife Bessie was there, too, along with Phil Silvers. The story goes that Bessie laughed at some joke Phil Silvers told and Silvers was watching her.

"Bessie with the laughing face," he said with a smile.

Van Heusen sat up. "Not a bad title for a song."

Johnny Burke yawned. He was the lyricist. They were all looking at him. "I'm tired. You guys do it."

And so Phil Silvers wrote the words while Van Heusen got a melody out of the piano in the next room. At a party on June 10, 1944, for Nancy Sinatra, Jr.'s, fourth birthday, they changed the Bessie to Nancy for the occasion—and, as they say, the rest is history. "Nancy (with the Laughing Face)" became one of Sinatra's biggest hits of the postwar era.

But 1944 was a year of many other personal triumphs for Frank Sinatra. The biggest of all was his trip to Washington, D.C., and when that occurred, Sinatra knew that he had really *arrived*.

It was Toots Shor, the New York nightclub owner, who was responsible for his trip to the nation's capital. Frank was always on the best of terms with Shor, and when Robert Hannegan, a Shor intimate and Democratic National Committee chairman, arranged for Shor to have tea with President Franklin D. Roosevelt, Sinatra was wide-eyed with envy.

Shor read the singer right. "I'd like to bring Sinatra," he told Hannegan.

It was arranged, and on September 28, 1944, Sinatra met the president with about twenty other people over tea in the White House. "Fainting, which once was so prevalent, has become a lost art among the ladies," the president was quoted as saying to Sinatra. "I'm glad that you have revived it."

Frank was in seventh heaven. He said that he felt as if he had seen a vision. "I thought, here is the greatest guy alive today and here's a little guy from Hoboken shaking his hand. He knows about everything, even my racket."

The media were not quite so enthralled. Some writers began screaming bloody murder. One pundit wrote that the Sinatra visit was a "cheap little publicity stunt." Washington politicians groused that the president had more important things to do than sit around talking with crooners and saloonkeepers.

Sinatra shrugged it all off. He continued to tell his friends that the president was "the kind of man you'd want for your father." His own son, Franklin Wayne, had been named for F.D.R., he pointed out. The upshot of the controversy was that Sinatra donated $7,500 to the Democratic party coffers. After all, his mother was an important member of the party in New Jersey.

Sinatra was at the top, but it was beginning to get a bit tough up there for him. Along with all the good things there were sinister rumblings—rumblings that Sinatra heard only faintly, and others not at all.

Already ugly rumors and stories about Sinatra's liaisons with Hollywood women—stars, starlets, and "others"—began to surface. In fact, columnists had a field day discussing the singer's extramarital cavortings.

Much of the running around had started during the filming of *Anchors Aweigh* in 1944 at MGM when Sinatra, in his sailor uniform, visited another set to chat with Lana Turner, the star of *Keep Your Powder Dry*, dressed up nicely in a tight-fitting WAC uniform. It was Turner who had invented the "sweater girl" image when someone suggested she take off the blouse under her sweater to see how she looked. Of course, she looked *great*. Turner had been hanging around with Turhan Bey, Robert Stack, and Peter Lawford, new arrivals in the film colony. Now she was suddenly being seen around town with Frank Sinatra. But Sinatra didn't limit himself to her. He was also going out with singer-actress Marilyn Maxwell, who was not nearly as big a movie star as Turner, but was a well-known personality in her own right and had a similar blond sex appeal.

Meanwhile, back home in New Jersey, Nancy Sinatra was becoming somewhat fretful over a marriage situation that now seemed quite shaky. With the movies taking up so much of Frank's time, Nancy decided that she and the two children would be much better off in California. So in the spring of 1944 Frank bought a place on Toluca Lake near Bing Crosby's home, and moved the Sinatra household there.

In that same year he made a special short film titled *The House I Live In,* a plea for tolerance. The story line, by screenwriter Albert Maltz, was simple. Coming out of a rehearsal, the singer finds a racially mixed group of youngsters fighting. He separates them, talks about prejudice and tolerance, and sings the song "The House I Live in," written by Earl Robinson and Lewis Allan. The critics applauded the film, and Sinatra was given a special Academy Award for it.

Things were still falling right for Frank in his singing career, too. In the fall of 1945, he premiered a CBS radio network show called "Songs by Sinatra," which, despite interruptions, would be on the air for two full years.

Hollywood was his oyster. He was a pal of "Prince" Mike Romanoff, the Beverly Hills restaurateur. New York was his oyster. The *New Yorker* began running E. J. Kahn's multi-part profile of him, later published as a book entitled *The Voice*.

And in Hollywood he was expanding his circle of friends—sometimes to include very big people indeed. Humphrey Bogart liked Sinatra from the first time he met him at the Players Restaurant on Sunset Strip.

"They tell me you have a voice that makes girls faint," Bogart said, as if speaking a line from one of his film scripts. "Make me faint."

Sinatra grinned and responded that he had an opening a week off and couldn't sing until that time. Bogart laughed. He liked Sinatra's cockiness and his irreverence toward the Hollywood establishment; both of these traits became evident as Sinatra continued his womanizing, in spite of the warnings of his publicist and the movie industry bigwigs he worked for.

Bogart affected an almost paternal role with Sinatra, and his warmth was reciprocated. In Bogart's presence, Sinatra was almost always on his best behavior and at his most charming.

But with others, it was not always so. He could turn instantly into a different person, becoming short-tempered and obnoxious. George Evans, his publicist, was becoming more and more concerned about his client's public image, which was beginning to self-destruct in front of his eyes.

Evans decided that the move of Nancy and the two young Sinatras to California might be a way to try to clean Frank's somewhat soiled image as a husband and father. Sinatra felt almost exactly the opposite: he didn't want to be thought of as a father or a husband. He was coming into his own swinging image, and he *liked* it. He was accumulating a group of his own friends now—men *and* women.

And so he began to have screaming sessions with Evans. He even got into a nasty argument with his good friend and mentor Toots Shor about Marilyn Maxwell during one of his engagements in New York. Sinatra wanted to take his blond friend out to a boxing match. Shor objected to their appearance in public together, saying that it would look as if he was abandoning Nancy, who was, after all, his wife. Sulking, Sinatra appeared at the fight with Marlene Dietrich and Joe DiMaggio, both of whom he had added to his growing list of celebrity friends.

But it wasn't just his problems with women that were beginning to cause trouble in his public life. He had other friends as well—some of whom had quite unsavory backgrounds. Of course, it was not unusual for singers and entertainers working in nightclubs and roadhouses to have friendships with gangsters and members of the underworld. Many such establishments were backed by mob money. But most entertainers allowed such acquaintances to lapse sooner or later, or at least kept them discreet and hidden from public view.

Sinatra was made of sterner stuff. Besides, he was Italian and of Sicilian extraction himself— perhaps making it all the easier for him to empathize with members of the so-called Mafia.

One of the top Mafia leaders in the United States— Salvatore Lucania, better known to the public as "Lucky" Luciano (note the different spelling of the family name)—had been deported to Italy to spend his remaining days in Naples. But he still held the reins of power in the Mafia and operated the U.S. "thing" (*cosa*) from Italy. In 1947, Luciano flew to Cuba—which had not yet fallen to Fidel Castro and was ruled by the notorious Fulgencio Batista (y Zaldivar), along with American mobsters—to see if he could work out a deal to get himself admitted back into the United States. With the big man himself—the *capo di tutti capi*—less than a hundred miles from American soil, every important hood in the vicinity made a point of flying down to Havana to pay their respects to Luciano.

Mobster Joseph (Doc) Stacher said that the Cuban meeting lasted a week, and everyone brought envelopes of tribute in cash to give to Luciano; as an exile, he was glad to get the money. But more important, the mobsters came to pay him their personal allegiance.

Frank Sinatra met two of the Fischetti brothers— Joseph and Rocco—in Miami and flew down with them to Havana. The Fischettis were cousins of Al Capone, the notorious Chicago gangster of the 1930s. There were actually three brothers, the third named Charles. But when Sinatra was seen in the company of any of the Fischettis, it was usually Joseph or Rocco. "The Italians among us were very proud of Frank," Stacher was quoted as saying in the book *Meyer Lansky*. "They always told me they had spent a lot of money helping him in his career, ever since he was with Tommy Dorsey's band. Lucky Luciano was very fond of Sinatra's singing."

Cuba was a haven for gangsters, gamblers, and almost anyone who wanted to have a bit of fun— illicit or otherwise—thanks to Santos Trafficante, a strong-arm mobster who was able to keep Batista's government minions at bay while carrying out the mob's specific operations. One of these operations was the staging of some of the most kinky sex shows ever seen anywhere in the Americas.

Luciano was ecstatic at the appearance of Sinatra in Cuba that year. Nothing was too good for the singer. His arrival had been trumpeted in the local press, and he attracted the attention of masses of Cubans as well as visiting Americans.

One day during Sinatra's visit to Havana, a nun ushered a group of Girl Scouts into the hotel where Sinatra was staying. They all wanted to see the famed Americano in person. Excited at the prospect of viewing Frank Sinatra in the flesh, they stole quietly along the corridor to the penthouse where he was registered. Barely able to restrain themselves from giggling in their excitement and anxiety, they found the suite door ajar. The nun peeked around the door into the room—and the blood drained from her face.

The Girl Scouts stood rooted to the spot. The penthouse was filled with bottles and lingerie, among which were half-naked bodies sprawled on the floor and draped over the sofas in every position imaginable—and some unimaginable.

Sinatra's presence in Havana with the mobsters did not remain a secret for long. In the last week of February 1947 columnist Robert Ruark of the Scripps-Howard chain ran a series of three columns, datelined Havana. It was a hatchet job aimed at Sinatra, not Luciano. "Sinatra was here [in Havana] for four days last week and during that time his companion in public and in private was Luciano, Luciano's bodyguards and a rich collection of gamblers and highbinders," Ruark wrote in his familiar hyperventilating prose. "The friendship was beautiful. They were seen together at the race track, the gambling casino and at special parties."

Ruark kept referring to Luciano as "Sinatra's boyfriend" and "Sinatra's buddy." "In addition to Mr. Luciano," he went on, referring to a party given the day before Sinatra returned to Miami, "I am told that Ralph Capone was present . . . and so was a rather large and well-matched assortment of the goons who find the south salubrious in the winter, or grand-jury time."

And there was more: "The curious desire to cavort among the scum is possibly permissible among citizens who are not peddling sermons to the nation's youth, and may even be allowed to a mealy-mouthed celebrity, if he is smart enough to confine his social tolerance to a hotel room. But Mr. Sinatra, the self-confessed savior of the country's small fry . . . seems to be setting a most-peculiar example for his hordes of pimply, shrieking slaves." Other columnists dug up more dirt. They wrote about the Fischettis, and about Sinatra's "command performance" before Luciano, and they certainly didn't leave out the gambling and drinking.

This noise died down after a while. Other things were more interesting to the public. But the media guns were not silent for long. In 1951, columnist Lee Mortimer of the *New York Mirror* resurrected the Cuba story and charged that Sinatra had actually gone to Havana not to cavort with the Fischettis, meet Luciano, and sing for the mobsters, but to deliver $2 million "in small bills" to Luciano, more or less as his "bag man" in the U.S.

As "proof," Mortimer noted that when Sinatra left the Miami–Havana plane in the company of the Fischettis he was carrying a valise. Stars of

Sinatra's prominence, he pointed out, did not usually carry their own hand luggage onto or off planes. In that satchel, Mortimer implied, lay the ill-gotten money for Luciano.

The response came from Sinatra in two 1952 stories in the *American Weekly,* initiated by a new press agent, Mack Miller, hired to prop up the sagging image of the singer. Here's how the answers to Mortimer's charges went: "Picture me, skinny Frankie, lifting two-million dollars in small bills. For the record, one thousand dollars in dollar bills weighs three pounds, which makes the load I am supposed to have carried six thousand pounds. Even assuming that the bills were twenties—the bag would still have required a couple of stevedores to carry it."

That was, of course, a classic rebuttal to Mortimer's hasty and ill-considered use of the word *small* in describing the bills allegedly in the satchel carried by Sinatra.

But there was more. Miller wanted Sinatra to lay it all on the line, and the text explained Sinatra's appearance in public with the Fischettis in this manner: "I was brought up to shake a man's hand when I am introduced to him without first investigating his past. Any report that I fraternized with goons or racketeers is a vicious lie."

He said that he had decided to visit Havana and Mexico City on vacation in 1947. On the way to Cuba he sang at a benefit for the Damon Runyon Cancer Fund in Miami, and it was there that he "ran into" Joe Fischetti, presumably among the guests at the benefit. Fischetti and his brothers were headed for Havana, and when he learned that

Sinatra was going to Cuba too, he switched his plane reservation to be with the singer.

In Cuba one night, Sinatra went on, he was at a bar with a New York restaurateur named Connie Immerman, where he met "a large group of men and women." Invited to dine with them, Sinatra suddenly "realized that one of the men in the party was Lucky Luciano." Although concerned that he might be letting himself in for criticism by staying with the group, he said that "he could think of no way to leave in the middle of the dinner without creating a scene."

Later that night Sinatra visited the jai alai games and toured the night spots, ending up at the Havana Casino—and there he "passed a table" where Luciano and others sat. When they invited Sinatra to join them, he "had a quick drink" and left. "These were the only times I've ever seen Luciano in my life," he wrote.

According to Nicholas Gage in *Mafia, U.S.A.*, FBI reports claimed that it was Rocco Fischetti, not Sinatra, who acted as bagman for Luciano, carrying $2 million in "very large bills" to the big boss—part of his income from the rackets. Mortimer had got the bag right, and the amount in the bag right, but not the identity of the bagman. Nevertheless, the harm was done. Although things calmed down for a while, Sinatra's connection with the mob had been planted in the public mind and was to remain there, festering, for several years.

In addition to problems with women and problems with underworld contacts, there were also problems with Sinatra's motion-picture career. Although *Anchors Aweigh* (1945) was a big hit and made MGM a pile of money, his next picture, *Till the*

Clouds Roll By (1946) was not a big winner; in that film he made only a cameo appearance as a guest star. *It Happened in Brooklyn* (1947), in which he starred opposite Kathryn Grayson, was not bad, but was by no means a smash success either.

By the time *The Miracle of the Bells* (1948) was released by RKO Pictures, it was obvious that Sinatra was on a downward slide in public esteem. He was not quite so convincing playing a Catholic priest as Bing Crosby had been several years earlier in *Going My Way*. His next film, *The Kissing Bandit* for MGM, was a real disaster, with a story that was too silly to be believed. It marked the nadir of his movie career.

Then came *Take Me Out to the Ball Game* (1949), which had Gene Kelly and Esther Williams to bolster him, and Sinatra singing a number of tunes. By the time he appeared in *On the Town* (1949), a big-budget movie version of the Broadway musical hit, he had been demoted in the credits to the Number Three spot (below Gene Kelly and Vera-Ellen)—not good for his ego. Even worse for his public image. And there was no help at all from his record sales, which were going the same way as his movie box-office receipts. Down and down.

From 1948 to 1951, Sinatra continued to make the *Billboard* charts, but he was never higher than Number Ten—he who was used to reigning supreme in the Number One spot. At the same time, he was declining dramatically in the annual *Down Beat* and *Metronome* polls as well.

He had introduced and popularized a new style of singing, but that trend, as all trends do, had begun to change. Another kind of song styling was coming into vogue. The hysteria and the shrieking were passé now, too. Maybe the psychologists were right about their being simply a sign of the wartime loneliness and malaise; anyway, things were different in the 1950s. The novelty of the microphone technique, as demonstrated by Bing Crosby and Frank Sinatra in particular, now became old hat. It was a whole new ballgame out there, with brand-new, and unknown, players. Frankie Laine, Johnny Ray, Eddie Fisher. These singers were belters who shouted the blues—from the rhythm-and-blues form—like the revivalists of the Old South.

Everything got louder; the healthier the belter, the greater his following. And, waiting in the wings, there was an even more formidable opponent of the pop-music ballad singer: the amplified group, which was epitomized by The Beatles.

But of course that is getting ahead of the story.

Sinatra's personal life was moving along as well as could be expected, given his busy professional schedule. On October 13, 1947, Hoboken, New Jersey, celebrated Frank Sinatra Day—in spite of the fact that Sinatra had deserted the New Jersey shores for the more salubrious coastline of California.

And the very next summer, his family was increased by the arrival of one more child—this one Christina, born at Cedars of Lebanon Hospital in Hollywood on June 20, 1948.

Yet in some ways, his personal life seemed to be slipping out of his control in an exorable manner. He had too many commitments to motion pictures, to the recording industry, to show business itself in all its phases. Besides that, he knew that he was beginning to be in trouble professionally.

There was one more important element in his life that contributed substantially to his slippage. It was his politics. When he originally arrived in Hollywood, Sinatra had been almost totally apolitical. But as he continued to work in show business, his social awareness widened; many of his co-workers were involved in political activity. The first time he appeared onstage with Sammy Davis, Jr., Sinatra demanded and got equal billing for the black performer—who subsequently became a close friend.

Sinatra's respect for his mother and her almost lifelong involvement in Democratic politics in New Jersey was another influence that helped to turn him into a political activist. After visiting with F.D.R. at the White House, Sinatra campaigned actively for his fourth presidential campaign.

As far back as 1944, when he had made *The House I Live In,* his political bias had become public knowledge. In general, it was this well-known fact that had helped rouse the ire of those members of the popular press who supported Republican and right-wing causes: for example, Robert Ruark, Westbrook Pegler, and Lee Mortimer, who all worked with newspapers and syndicates—Hearst and Scripps-Howard—that represented the Republicans, not the Democrats and the New Deal. Robert Ruark's information about Sinatra's trip to Havana was said to have been leaked deliberately to the columnist by Henry Anslinger, the chief of the Federal Narcotics Bureau, who, it was said, was convinced that Sinatra was a political "pinko."

Sinatra was also named in 1949 by the California State Senate Committee on Un-American Activities as being among prominent figures who had supposedly "followed or appeased some of the Communist party-line program over a long period of time."

"This statement," Sinatra shot back, "is the product

of liars, and liars do make very un-American leaders."

And that was another problem Sinatra was beginning to have—real trouble with the media. And this wasn't all political. Some of it was personal.

Because of his extramarital adventures in Hollywood, Sinatra had incurred the wrath of such powerful women in the press as Hedda Hopper and Louella Parsons, the Hollywood gossip queens, and Dorothy Kilgallen. Hopper and Parsons continually goaded him about his affairs. Kilgallen seemed annoyed at him for her own personal reasons—specifically for his disparaging public remarks about her receding chin. Since she considered herself quite attractive and was, like most people, rather vain, Sinatra's remarks hurt her. Naturally, she got back at him whenever she could.

But there was one columnist with whom Sinatra tangled in 1947 who more or less became the keystone in the large funereal arch Sinatra seemed to be erecting over himself. In a way, it wrote "paid" to all the sarcasm, bitterness, grumbling, and personal vindictiveness his friends and associates had been noticing in him for the past five years. Sinatra had been struggling against adverse fortune for several years—struggling ineffectually, as it turned out. It was Lee Mortimer's columns that graveled Sinatra the most. "I will belt him sometime!" he told Earl Wilson in a rage.

Nobody took him seriously. Sure, he kept trim. But he was a spindly guy. Not a bruiser.

One of Sinatra's buddies in his New York nightclub adventures was a violinist named Joe Candullo. Candullo was a friend of Mortimer's as well as Sinatra's. "Give Mortimer a message," Sinatra told

Candullo. "If you don't quit knocking me and my fans, I'm going to knock your brains out." Candullo refused to deliver the message. It seemed pretty silly to him. Sinatra kept at him. "He hangs out at the China Doll. Right?"

Candullo admitted that.

"Take me over there and point him out to me. I'll give it to him. Just let me know it's him, and I'll take care of him."

Candullo shook his head. "Don't do it, Frank!"

"I'm doing it," Sinatra insisted.

Candullo delivered the message. Mortimer grinned when he heard it. "I'm not afraid of him! I'm not going to stop writing about him either. Tell that to him and his cheap hoodlums."

Mortimer's next column appeared with a paragraph that said the dishwasher, the busboy, and the cleanup woman sang better than Frank Sinatra. "He doesn't scare me," Mortimer assured Candullo.

It was April 8, 1947. The scene had shifted to the West Coast. Ciro's on the Sunset Strip was one of the most popular places in Hollywood. Actually, it wasn't in Hollywood, in Beverly Hills, *or* in Los Angeles. The "Strip" was an area that because of a surveyor's correction belonged to no known community and was by default county land. For that reason the clubs operating there could get away with things that other nearby clubs under the control of the various city police departments couldn't. At that time the Strip was the Gold Coast for entertainers and the Hollywood gadabouts. By utter coincidence, both Lee Mortimer and Frank Sinatra happened to be having dinner that night at Ciro's. Each was surrounded by a large entourage of friends and hangers-on.

Though ensconced amid friends, each became aware of the presence of the other. As in most of Sinatra's public and physical encounters, there were two sides to the story.

Sinatra's Version

As he prepared to leave with his friends, Frank was feeling friendly and amiable and decided to nod his greetings to Mortimer across the room. As he did so, he noticed that the columnist did not nod in recognition but reciprocated with a "drop dead" look.

Mortimer's Version

As he was leaving the nightclub for the street with his friends, Mortimer saw Sinatra jump up from his table and deliberately barge out into the foyer to clip Mortimer on the back, sneering out: "Next time I'll kill you, you degenerate!" And with that, three of Sinatra's paid bodyguards leaped on Mortimer and threw him to the floor, beating him with their fists.

Sinatra's Version (cont'd)

Quote by Sinatra: "He called me a dago. I saw red. I was all mixed up from being called a dago."

Mortimer's Version (cont'd)

Mortimer claimed he had never used any such language. In fact, he didn't even know that Sinatra was in the nightclub until his three bruisers swarmed all over him.

Known for Fact

Sinatra brushed himself off after the battle and went back into the dining room. Mortimer was hurt and called a doctor and a lawyer. His doctor discovered wrist and neck bruises and evidence of a blow behind the ear. The columnist then swore out a warrant for the arrest of the singer on assault-and-battery charges.

The following afternoon, as Sinatra was rehearsing at a radio station for a show, two Beverly Hills policemen came in and placed him under arrest. They took him to the Beverly Hills District Court, where he pleaded not guilty to a charge of battery and requested a jury trial.

Bail was set at $500.

There was a funny smile on Sinatra's face as he went quickly through his pockets and failed to come up with enough cash to cover his bail. From spectators, hangers-on, lawyers—and even his nemeses, grinning reporters—he got enough to avoid spending the night in the clink.

The trial was going to be a serious one. Sinatra faced a possible six months in jail if the judgment went against him. The district attorney's office investigated and felt that Sinatra had been wrong in jumping the newspaperman. It was determined that Sinatra had been the attacker.

"Did you have to hit him?" Earl Wilson asked Sinatra.

"He was coming toward me. I thought he was going to hit me," Sinatra said.

"He said you belted him from behind."

"I hit him on the chin! To hit him on the chin and hit him from behind, you've got to be an acrobat."

Louis B. Mayer, who had him under contract, had the last word for Sinatra. "Settle the damned thing."

It was not that easy. On June 4, 1947, Sinatra

and Mortimer faced each other in the district court in Beverly Hills.

Sinatra's Courtroom Statement

He stated that the incident had occurred when an acquaintance stopping by his table at Ciro's claimed that Mortimer had made a remark that was offensive to Sinatra. On further inquiry, however, the singer had discovered that Mortimer had made no such remark. No provocation had existed for the fisticuffs that followed. Sinatra expressed keen regret over the incident.

Mortimer's Courtroom Statement

He expressed satisfaction with the apology. He was gratified when Sinatra publicly acknowledged that he had not been called any vile names by Mortimer. The district attorney requested a withdrawal of the charges. Mortimer consented.

Results of Trial

Sinatra paid court costs of fifty dollars, and the judge dismissed the case. The trial took all of six minutes.

Out of court, Sinatra paid Mortimer $9,000. His total costs, including attorney fees, amounted to over $25,000 out of Sinatra's pocket.

"It was a pleasure to pay it," Sinatra said later.

Mortimer was not so sanguine. "What hurts most is having to go through life admitting Sinatra knocked me down."

Mortimer was later punched by *another* nightclub figure, and newspaper stories said, tongue-in-cheek, that "the list of suspects had been narrowed down to thousands."

Sinatra came out of the affair a lot worse off than Mortimer. The public was not on his side anymore, either, especially in these altercations with the press. It seemed to be saying, "Good-bye, Frank." Everything he had worked so hard for seemed to be slipping through his fingers.

He began looking up old friends, going out late at night, arguing with his associates, drinking too much. Many of his friends didn't want to see him. They were turning their backs on him.

By 1952, Sinatra was at the bottom of the pile—so far down and so far out that he didn't even know exactly where he was or what had happened to him. Columbia Records had dropped him. He had made a deal with ABC-TV—but that had died on the vine. There were no offers from film companies for roles. He did get a couple of dogs—*Double Dynamite* in 1951 and *Meet Danny Wilson* in 1952—but they were nothing to write home about. Even M.C.A. —the colossus of all agencies—dropped him.

When he appeared at the New York Paramount in an attempt to revive his career, he got precious little help from the media. GONE ON FRANKIE IN '42; GONE IN '52, read one headline. The subhead said it all: WHAT A DIFFERENCE A DECADE MAKES—EMPTY BALCONY. Outside the theater a friend heard three girls at the stage door murmuring, "Frankie!" When the friend asked how they liked Frankie, one of them replied: "Frankie Laine, he's wonderful!"

"I'm mad about him," the other said—but *him* turned out to be Johnny Ray!

In those first few dark years of the 1950s, Sinatra had become entangled in an affair of the heart that almost took him over completely and buried him.

At the least, it dominated his life for three mad years.

It had begun in New York one night in December 1949, when he had run into Ava Gardner at the preview of a new movie, *Gentlemen Prefer Blondes*. From that moment on he began seeing her on a more or less steady basis—while at the same time he was trying to sort out his own life.

Not exactly the easiest of chores to take on simultaneously.

★ 5 ★

Ave, Ava!

Ava Gardner was a smoldering, sensual, and extremely beautiful Hollywood star in the Metro-Goldwyn-Mayer firmament. Born in Boon Hill, North Carolina, she had grown up in the Deep South as the youngest of a family of seven children—cared for mostly by her sister Beatrice, who was almost twenty years older than she.

Reared in poverty, Ava was in the habit of making herself fade into the background as much as possible. As she matured, it became obvious that she would be a lovely woman, the only daughter in the Gardner clan with dark hair and green eyes—the last, her most interesting feature, inherited from her Irish father.

At the height of the Depression, her mother and father split up, the father remaining in Boon Hill to serve as a sawmill supervisor and her mother moving to Newport News, Virginia, to operate a rooming house. Three of the Gardner girls were married or on their own by now, and seven-year-old Ava accompanied her mother, with her unmarried sister joining her living brother—the other had died accidentally from an exploding rifle shell—to live with their father. Those who knew her in Newport News remember Ava as an awkward and surly girl who was unusually withdrawn.

Wearing hand-me-down clothes and speaking in a heavy hillbilly drawl, she seemed to flaunt her insecurity and awkwardness and resist any possible friendships. One talent she had in plenty: the ability to use fluently all the four-letter words in the English language.

Ava's oldest sister Beatrice—known as Bappie—was nineteen years old when Ava was born. She married a New York photographer named Lawrence Tarr, and Ava eventually went to live with the Tarrs when her father died and her mother became terminally ill.

Tarr was in the habit of showcasing photographs of Ava—among other people—in front of his shop, and it was there that a runner for the legal department of MGM's New York office spotted her. Pretending to be a "talent scout," he called for a date with her, but Bappie intercepted the call. The upshot of this incident was that pictures of Ava were sent to MGM in Hollywood, a screen test was made—without dialogue, to mask the fact that Ava's speech was impossibly Southern—and Ava was eventually sent for by MGM and signed up to a standard seven-year contract. Louis B. Mayer saw her test and was said to have remarked: "She can't talk. She can't act. She's terrific. Sign her."

Easily adapting herself to the life-style of the motion-picture world, Ava appeared in several short MGM walk-on scenes, aroused the ardor of Mickey Rooney, and married him. Doomed from the start, the marriage disintegrated when Ava became interested in other men, including Artie Shaw, who distinguished himself by marrying several Hollywood starlets and other movie beauties, among them Lana Turner, a friend of Ava's on the MGM lot.

Meanwhile Ava's acting career was blooming. She made her name in *Whistle Stop* and was even better in *The Killers*. It was her personal life that was all mixed up and complicated. And marrying Shaw didn't help matters. The Shaw marriage was shaky from the start. In a year and six days, divorce put an end to it. Ava began dating Howard Hughes, whom she had gone out with before meeting Shaw. Hughes had more money than anybody else on the Hollywood scene. Then came Robert Mitchum . . .

In fact, it was to teach Mitchum a lesson—since he had told her again and again that he wouldn't marry her—that Ava left him in November 1949, during a Chicago promotion jaunt for one of his pictures, and went to New York, where she attended the premiere of *Gentlemen Prefer Blondes* and left it with another MGM property—Frank Sinatra.

Later, at the party for the cast, Ava and Frank were together constantly, laughing and seemingly having the time of their lives.

A week or two later, the two of them were together once again at a birthday party given for Sinatra at the Copacabana by its manager, Jack Entratter. At the time, Ava was scheduled to begin shooting a new MGM picture, *Pandora and the Flying Dutchman,* but it was postponed until James Mason, who was to play the Dutchman, could finish another movie.

Ava stayed in New York.

She and Sinatra spent much of their time together until just after the New Year, when Sinatra was signed to a two-week inaugural engagement at the newly built Shamrock Hotel in Houston. This was a mammoth pile, covering seven acres of grounds, with guest rooms hung with expensive oil paintings and a luxurious penthouse that went for $2,100 a month—big money in those days.

By now Sinatra realized that Ava Gardner meant something to him. He could not stand to have her out of his sight. And so he invited her to go to the big opening in Houston with him. She hesitated. There was a morals clause in her MGM contract, and she was in enough trouble already with her two failed marriages. In New York she and Frank had managed to maintain a low profile, going out together almost every night, but not showing up at highly publicized spots. In Houston it might be a different story.

Playing it by the book because of her contract, she contacted MGM for permission to go to Houston. Eddie Mannix, who was the second-in-command at Metro, refused her request. She went over his head to Louis B. Mayer himself, who also said no. In fact, he said a lot more than that, calling her every name in the book, and more—but in a nice way, of course.

She made up her mind. "Neither Metro nor the newspapers nor anyone else is going to run my life!"

She took the plane to Houston to join Sinatra.

From a public-relations standpoint, this was a serious gaffe. The lavish inauguration ceremonies at the Shamrock brought photographers from all the magazines and newspapers in the country, and some from abroad. They kept watches, trying to spot Sinatra and Gardner together. It became a game of hide-and-seek.

One night the two of them were having what they hoped would be a quiet dinner at Vincent's Restaurant as guests of the mayor, when a photographer for the *Houston Post* was tipped off by columnist Bill Roberts. The photographer, Edward Schisser, came over to take a picture of them as they sat eating spaghetti together.

Schisser asked Sinatra if he could get a picture.

"Beat it, you bum," Sinatra told him automatically.

Schisser did not beat it. He simply stood there and adjusted his lens. Sinatra leaped up and made a grab for the camera. Then he attempted to punch Schisser. Ava screamed and put her hands over her eyes. Sinatra sank down beside her, aware that he had done a dumb thing. Now the columist had his story—not only were Sinatra and Ava Gardner "together," but they were obviously intent on not letting it be known.

"I refused graciously," Sinatra explained later about the incident with Schisser.

From that moment on, the Houston idyll disintegrated. Frank and Ava's cover was blown. Wherever they went, they were in full sight of the press. What had started out to be a private affair had by now turned into an open scandal. Rumors of Sinatra's shaky marriage were exhumed, dusted off, and reprinted, with additional speculation, including Ava items, to embellish them. To make matters worse, Sinatra learned that his old friend and publicist George Evans had died of a heart attack in New York. Sinatra was very close to Evans, the man who had created the singer's swoon image; he flew to New York for the funeral, leaving Ava in Houston.

In New York he was told another devastating piece of news. Mannie Sachs, his best and most supportive friend in the recording world, was resigning from Columbia Records, which still had Sinatra under contract. The man he was going to be working with—the man who was taking Sach's place—was Mitch Miller.

When Sinatra flew back to the Coast, he discovered that things were even worse there. MGM was beginning to negotiate with M.C.A., Sinatra's agents, to break his movie contract, requesting the sum of $85,000 as the kiss-off.

As for his marriage, Sinatra learned that Nancy was upset by the news of the affair with Ava—as well she might be. The honorable thing to do was ask for a divorce, which he did. She refused, pointing out that her religion forbade divorce. Of course Sinatra was Catholic too, and he felt that old Catholic guilt rise to torment him. This made his affair with Ava more tenuous and frustrating. Their relationship suffered and they saw less and less of one another.

And suddenly Frank was having trouble with his voice. George Evans had once told him that his voice problems were caused by what we now call stress, but what Evans then picturesquely called "guilt germs."

The story of the Sinatra–Gardner relationship was in the papers every day. MGM began to receive hate mail. Ava was terribly upset when she began getting missives calling her "Jezebel," "bitch," etc. She even got violently threatening anonymous phone calls.

Sinatra was scheduled to sing at the Copacabana in New York throughout March; he wanted Ava with him. To get back at the critics who had been saying that he was losing his voice and that his style was out of fashion, Sinatra wore a coonskin cap, swung a whip, and blew a duck call to satirize "Mule Train" and "The Cry of the Goose"—pop songs sung by Frankie Laine, who was then the leader in the pop song charts.

Ava appeared at the opening in a no-shoulder gown, and clapped loudly for Sinatra. It was a tough evening—one of the toughest openings Sinatra had ever had. When he approached the bandstand, it seemed as if he might not make it at all. His hands were shaking so much everyone in the club noticed. Ava realized at once that the vibes were bad: the audience had not come to listen to Sinatra sing but to see him take a nosedive right in the spotlight of the entertainment world. She closed her eyes and crossed her fingers for him.

When he came to "Nancy with the Laughing Face," Ava flushed deep red. She could hear snickers from the sophisticates in the audience. She lifted her head and tried to bluff it through the set, but inside she was doing a slow burn.

Later that night she confronted Sinatra: "Did you *have* to sing that fucking song? It made me feel like a real fool!"

"It's been a good-luck song for me for years," Sinatra replied innocently. "I sing it in almost every big show."

Ava glowered. "Don't expect me to sit out there and get laughed at every night. Either the song goes, or *I* go."

He dropped the song from the set.

The reviews of the opening weren't all that good, anyway. "He's using stunts to conceal the fact that his voice has slipped," one reviewer said. "He's letting the orchestra drown out his inability to reach the romantic peaks in his songs."

"Bullshit!" retorted Sinatra.

Ava continued to visit the Copa every night to hear Sinatra sing, and slowly members of Frank's inner circle began to come back to see him and talk to him. One of them, Rocco Fischetti, was sitting in the audience one night and Ava introduced a friend of hers to him. He began taking her out. Sometimes Ava accompanied the two of them. One night Fischetti got into an argument with Ava's friend, and in a blind fury threw a cup of hot coffee in her face, right in front of Ava. Ava stalked out in a rage, cursing him out as she did so. Now she began to get on Frank about his so-called friends, particularly the Chicago hoods that he had known ever since he had started singing professionally. Sinatra listened to her diatribes in stony silence.

Later on, Ava discovered that Frank had received a telegram from another Hoboken friend of his, the man known as Willie Moore, a.k.a. Willie Moretti— the New Jersey Mafia boss. When she found the wire and read it, she blew up.

It said:

I AM VERY MUCH SURPRISED WHAT I HAVE BEEN READING IN THE NEWSPAPERS BETWEEN YOU AND YOUR DARLING WIFE. REMEMBER YOU HAVE A DECENT WIFE AND CHILDREN. YOU SHOULD BE VERY HAPPY. REGARDS TO ALL. WILLIE MOORE.

This near-illiterate communiqué was too much for Ava. Here was a known hood, a professional killer, a man with no regard for the law of the land—and *he* had the nerve to chide a law-abiding citizen about his plans to divorce his wife and marry someone else! The implication that Moretti was *better* than Sinatra because he was still married to the same woman and had children by her cut Ava to the quick.

She let loose at Frank and spoke in no uncertain terms about his penchant for hanging around with the wrong kind of people—types who could do no good to his image. She said a lot of his friends came from unsavory backgrounds and were giving him a bad name by being seen with him. She wanted him to quit associating with members of the underworld; if he didn't, she implied, he would be making a choice between them and her.

Sinatra was indeed in a black mood as he listened to her rail at him. Finally he held up his hand, his face stony and his eyes flashing blue danger. "Don't cut corners too close on me, baby," he snapped, and walked away stiffly.

Moretti, incidentally, was not far from his own end at the time. His mental health endangered by an advanced case of syphilis, he was shortly afterward gunned down by a fellow Mafioso to prevent him from talking.

Frustrated and concerned about the way things were going with Frank, Ava hardly knew where to turn. Learning that Artie Shaw, her favorite ex-husband, was in town, she looked him up and began unloading her troubles on him. "He wants to marry me," Ava told Shaw.

"What about you?" Shaw asked. "Do you want to marry him?"

"I've got to," Ava said tightly.

"What do you mean, 'got to'?"

"How would it look if I didn't?" Ava wondered

aloud. "I pulled him away from Nancy. Now he's having a tough time. I've just got to, that's all."

Later on, Shaw visited the Copa and sat with Ava to watch the show. After his set, Sinatra sat down with them. He stared at Shaw coldly. "I don't think you should be seeing Ava," he told him in a soft, somewhat menacing voice. "You're divorced, you know."

Shaw was startled by Sinatra's belligerence. He gazed around meaningfully. "Are you as tough as you sound?"

"Yeah."

Shaw smiled faintly. He turned to the heavy-set bodyguard standing behind Sinatra's chair. "Then why do you need him?"

Sinatra simply stared into the distance. Shaw soon left.

Now the columnists were tormenting Ava about her relationship with Sinatra. They were writing about her as a home wrecker, just as she had suspected they would when she began going out with him. "What are you going to do about it?" one writer asked her.

"Since Frank is still officially married," she responded with admirable calm, "it would be in the worst possible taste to discuss any further plans. One thing I'm sure of is that Frank's plans to leave Nancy came into his life long before I ever did."

In spite of her cool answer—probably something she had dreamed up with the help of a friend or publicity associate—she was furious at the press and unhappy with Sinatra's Sicilian friends who always seemed to be hanging around.

When she confided in Artie Shaw and said she would like to meet some "normal" people in New

York, he invited Sinatra and Ava to a dinner party that included some of his more intellectual friends. Sinatra did not appear that night. Ava came alone, saying in a low voice that something had come up and that Frank couldn't come. What she didn't tell Shaw was that Sinatra had *ordered* her not to go to the party herself.

During the dinner party the telephone rang. It was for Ava. She got on the phone. "Well," said Frank on the other end of the line. "I just called to say good-bye."

"Where are you going, Frank?" Ava asked in all innocence. "Why can't I come, too?"

"Not where I'm going, baby," Sinatra said coolly.

Ava was shocked to hear the sound of a pistol shot, followed by a short silence, and then a second shot.

After a seemingly endless cab ride, Ava finally arrived at the Hampshire House, where she and Frank were staying, and rushed up to their room. A crowd was milling about the hallway outside his door. Two firemen were there, wielding axes to break down the door, which, they said, was bolted from inside. David Selznick, who had the next-door suite, said that he had heard shots and had reported them to the hotel management. Then the firemen had appeared. "I think the son of a bitch just shot himself!" he told Ava.

When the firemen finally broke down the door, they surged into the suite where they found a pale-faced and morose Frank Sinatra sitting on the bed in his pajamas. He was obviously unhurt. There was no pistol in sight.

"We heard shots," one of the hotel guests said.

"I never fired any shots," said Sinatra, looking around slowly.

"But you *called* me!" Ava protested.

"Then I went right to bed. Next thing I know, you're all breaking down the door and overrunning the place!"

His face was getting grim.

Gradually calm was restored and the entrance sealed off for repairs. Ava could guess what had happened. She had left him to go to Artie Shaw's for dinner and Sinatra was in a rage. He was just doing this to get back at her.

After this dramatic set-to hit the newspapers, Ava began to get more hate mail—this time addressed to her at the hotel. Some of the letter writers even claimed that they knew she was pregnant— with Sinatra's child! How they knew, they never said. They accused Ava of ruining Nancy Sinatra's life. They accused her of everything. She was bitterly frustrated and unhappy.

Work might be the tonic for her troubles. She decided to fly to Spain on March 26, 1950, two weeks before shooting started on *Pandora and the Flying Dutchman*. At least she wouldn't have to see Sinatra's Sicilian friends and the singer's morose countenance.

The filming of the picture took an incredible fifteen weeks. And now there were rumors about goings-on in Spain as well as in New York. In Spain they focused around Ava and her co-star. Although James Mason was in the picture, it was a Spanish bullfighter named Mario Cabre who was Ava's lover in the film. The rumors had it that off-camera as well as on-camera, Ava and Cabre had a great thing going.

When this news surfaced in New York, Frank's friends heard about it first and took it to him immediately. At the outset Frank was able to dismiss the story and pretend it was nothing.

Every day he and Ava had transatlantic phone conversations, exchanging bits of gossip and white lies. Then the idea of Ava and the bullfighter took hold with the MGM studio publicists, and much was made of their relationship in the media. The studio was still not sold on the Sinatra–Gardner engagement, and the brass was doing everything it could, secretly, to break it up. The Barcelona bullfighter seemed to be the answer to the problem; *he* might be able to drive a wedge between The Voice and The Look.

"Studio publicity!" was how Ava dismissed Frank's angry allusion to Spain and that bullfighter. Sinatra knew exactly how to treat this problem. He began going out on the town with his old friend Marilyn Maxwell. In a complete turnaround of his normal press relationship, he invited photographers to take good close-ups of them in various haunts. These pictures began appearing in newspapers and magazines in Spain as well as in New York.

The telephone calls became long recitals of what Sinatra was doing to while away the time—naming names, places, and even menus in some cases.

"I won't stand much more of this!" Ava would shout and start to curse. Absence was not making either heart grow fonder. And then, abruptly, the story took two sudden, and frightening, new twists.

Ironically, the first turn was a happy one for Sinatra. Nancy relented—to a degree—by agreeing to give her husband a separation. Not a divorce, but a separation. She filed for separate maintenance in

Santa Monica District Court on April 26, 1950. At first Sinatra was elated at his wife's decision; he knew that she would eventually agree to divorce him so that he could marry Ava Gardner. But quite quickly depression set in. The break with Nancy was not as simple as he had anticipated. He began suffering from George Evans's "guilt germs."

Thus:

On the night of that same day, April 26, 1950, Frank Sinatra opened his mouth to start singing at the Copacabana—and nothing came out.

"Nothing but dust," as one associate put it.

For the first time, Frank Sinatra had actually lost his voice *completely*. His trouble was eventually diagnosed by Dr. Irving Goldman as a submucosal hemorrhage of the throat. According to the story in the newspapers, Sinatra was ordered to take a two-week rest. As it turned out, it was forty days—not fourteen days—before he could sing again. The forced vacation was a traumatic one. Sinatra truly thought that he had lost that golden voice of his forever. Yet he was jaunty and in good spirits when he turned up at the airport to fly down to Miami Beach for a little rest and recreation.

On hearing the news of his voice loss, Ava telephoned him, but the conversation was not entirely satisfactory. Sinatra could barely make himself heard over the wire. Instead of talking, he played his latest album for Ava—which did little to reassure her.

On the eighth day of his enforced rest in Miami, and against Dr. Goldman's orders for complete rest, Sinatra booked passage to London, and there chartered a plane to Barcelona. He was going to see Ava—or else.

On May 10 he staggered into Ava's villa, carrying six bottles of Coca-Cola and a big pack of Wrigley's chewing gum. He also brought a Van Cleef & Arpels diamond necklace.

It was all fun and games after that—for a while. But pretty soon the situation degenerated into another harangue about the bullfighter. "If I hear that Spanish runt has been hanging around you again, I'll kill him *and* you!" That was Sinatra, trying to get his voice back in shape again.

"We're in a fucking movie together!" shouted Ava. "He's *supposed* to be my lover. How can he avoid being near me? Besides, I haven't raised hell about Marilyn—have I?"

"That's different," Sinatra growled. "We're old friends."

"Mario and I," Ava said stiffly, "are *new* friends."

New friends or old friends, Sinatra and Ava were either at one another's lips or at one another's throats during the remainder of Sinatra's visit. Soon he flew off to Paris, en route to Los Angeles to complete his vacation out on the Coast.

The press was in hot pursuit. Earl Wilson reached Ava and asked her if Sinatra had flown to Paris in a huff because the Spanish bullfighter was issuing bulletins about Ava's love for him. "Honey, it's all a big lie!" Ava told him. "He left because he's got to get back to a TV show. We're closer than we've ever been."

Wilson wanted to check out whether or not Sinatra had brought her a necklace worth $10,000. "Holy Christ, Frank brought me six bottles of Coca-Cola and some chewing gum!" snapped Ava. In response to the questions about her "affair" with Cabre, Ava growled: "I'll kill those bastards! They take what's happening in the picture and pretend it's really going on."

Sinatra was beginning to feel like a ping-pong ball—batted between two separate and equally angry players. When he was with Ava, all they did was quarrel and then make up. The lovers did manage a few good months in the summer of 1950 in London, when Sinatra was a big hit at the Palladium.

Once back in California, he *again* confronted Nancy for some kind of agreement that would include divorce, not just separation. By now the Sinatras were living on North Carolwood Drive, in the Holmby Hills section of Los Angeles, on a rambling three-acre estate purchased in 1949. Sinatra had his own place in Coldwater Canyon, plus a palatial "hideaway" in Palm Springs for weekends and vacations.

On September 18, 1950, Nancy did win her separate-maintenance suit, was awarded one-third of Sinatra's annual salary, got control of the house in Holmby Hills, and was awarded custody of the three children.

But the formal granting of this separation did not clear the air at all between Ava and Frank. Their relationship continued its on-again off-again nature. Walter Winchell even printed an item to the effect that Sinatra had tried to commit suicide. The story was traced to an unidentified friend who had had him taken to a hospital after discovering him in the elevator of his apartment building with blood seeping out of his slit wrists.

There was more. Mannie Sachs told Earl Wilson that he had gone to the Sinatra apartment in the Hampshire House one day "and found Frank with his head in the oven." Whether Sachs meant this literally or figuratively is not known. Later on a notice appeared in the paper that Frank Sinatra had been firing a revolver into his mattress at the Hampshire House. "I think he was doing that shooting and oven stuff just to scare Ava," Mannie told a friend. "The shooting wasn't *at* anybody, just to make some noise."

The relationship between Ava and Frank had deteriorated seriously. They were constantly at each other's throat. At one memorable point, Sinatra made up with her by presenting her with two gorgeous Welsh corgis. It has been said that from that date on, Ava was almost always seen with one of those dogs.

Nancy persisted in opposing divorce, even as Frank pressed her harder. Ava challenged him: he wasn't *trying* hard enough, damn it! She set up a barrier. She wouldn't even see him unless he obtained that divorce. The lovers fought bitterly all through the winter of 1950–51—sometimes in private, sometimes in public. In March 1951 Sinatra made one of his most emotional recordings—"I'm a Fool to Want You"—reflective of his own inner turmoil.

Finally, in late spring 1951, Nancy broke down. Knowing at this point that there was no way back for her and Frank, she agreed to a divorce. "I'm convinced," she told Louella Parsons, "that a divorce is the only way for my happiness as well as Frank's."

Yet it took more than two months for Sinatra to make the move—which he did on August 18, filing for divorce in Reno, Nevada, where he was appearing at the time at the Riverside Inn. "Miss Gardner and I will definitely be married," he said.

Even the filing of the suit failed to clear the air

entirely between the lovers. Ava was having her troubles with the studio, but it was her affair with Frank that was eating her up inside. On September 26, 1951, she collapsed at MGM studios in West Hollywood. She was rushed to the hospital with what was diagnosed as a severe virus infection. For three weeks she lay helpless, with Sinatra all the way across the country in New York fulfilling a singing engagement.

She revived in due time and finally joined Frank in New York on October 28. And then, on November 1, news came through that the divorce Frank had filed for in August had become official and the two of them immediately flew to Las Vegas for the final hearing.

Within twenty-four hours of the decree, Sinatra and Ava were trying to get married in Philadelphia, where the waiting-time laws were less strict than in New York. But Philadelphia's period was three days, and there seemed to be no way to circumvent it. Sinatra was furious; Ava surly. As they met reporters and photographers on their return to New York, one cried out: "Let's have a wedding-day smile, Mr. Sinatra. Kiss the bride, Mr. Sinatra. Just once, Mr. Sinatra."

"Get out of my way, you sons of bitches!" Frank shouted, and fought his way through the crowd with Ava in tow.

"Christ, why are we always on the run?" Ava cried as she dove into the back of a cab and sank down in frustration.

They ate dinner that night at the Hampshire House with James and Pamela Mason. Frank happened to smile faintly at a woman dining at a nearby table. Ava glowered at him. "I can't even trust him on the eve of our wedding!" she snapped at the Masons.

By the time they got up to their suite the lovers were quarreling loudly and violently. Once inside, Ava was so furious that she threw her diamond necklace out the window, pushed Sinatra out of the bedroom, and locked the door against him.

Nevertheless, the wedding was still on. It finally took place on November 7 in Philadelphia at the home of Lester Sachs, a cousin of Mannie Sachs. The Sinatras had a brief honeymoon—one day in Florida, four days in Cuba, and then back to New York. At the airport, there were reporters again—everywhere.

The dialogue went like some sort of stylized ritual, strophe by antistrophe.

"Where are you going to stay, Mr. Sinatra?"

"None of your damned business."

"Where are your boxing gloves, Mr. Sinatra?"

"That's a funny line. Very funny. Ha-ha."

"Are you in trim?"

"If you were my age and weight, I could take you."

"What do you weigh?"

"I think I can show you."

Less than a fortnight after their wedding, while the newlyweds were in Sinatra's house in Palm Springs, they began fighting again. It got so bad that Ava ran out of the house and drove off to the desert to cool down.

At eight the next morning the phone rang in Artie Shaw's Manhattan Apartment. "I'm leaving!" he heard Ava shouting at him across the country. "I'm going back to L.A.!"

"Cutting out for good?" Shaw wanted to know.

"Well, no. But I can't handle it—it's fucking impossible!"

"We all know that. Give it two months and it'll get worse."

In December Sinatra and Ava flew to London, where Sinatra sang at a big charity show attended by the British royal family. Ava enjoyed speaking to the Duke of Edinburgh, and Sinatra traded insults with the press, argued with the orchestra during rehearsals, and received a decidedly tepid reception for his chores.

To cap it, when they returned to their rented apartment in London, they discovered that thieves had broken in and stolen Frank's cameo cufflinks and a platinum-and-sapphire ring.

But, worse than that, and somehow symbolic of the whole garbled mess—Ava's diamond-and-emerald necklace was gone.

★ 6 ★

Farewell, My Lovely

The Sinatra–Gardner marriage was, like the Sinatra–Gardner romance, fraught with ironies and contradictions. The courtship took so long to be consummated by marriage that the two principals were ready to split up by the time their relationship was formalized.

Oh, they were in love. There was no question about that. Years later Ava Gardner was to tell a journalist that she *still* loved Frank Sinatra—"and I always will." And she concluded by pointing out: "Our trouble was that we couldn't live together."

Their marriage only continued and exacerbated the quarrels that had come to epitomize their love-hate relationship. Ava complained about Frank's outbursts against the news media; she talked about his penchant for decking photographers whenever he could. She didn't like the bitchy mood he exhibited when he was in public and around journalists.

He brought up the subject of Artie Shaw and complained about Ava's continued relationship with him. He groused about Mickey Rooney. He griped about Howard Hughes. He watched every move she made in public, especially when men were around.

She got at him about Lana Turner and Marilyn Maxwell and dozens of other women he had known, knew, or was about to know.

It went around and around.

Their professional commitments made it impossible for them to work and live together at the same time. They were apart too much for any kind of sustained relationship. Besides, Sinatra was suffering from those "guilt germs"—worrying still about having left Nancy. Things were falling apart all around him.

And they were falling apart around Ava, too. She later analyzed her own problem with men generally. "Each time I married, I really thought and hoped it would be for good. The trouble was that the men all married Ava Gardner, the so-called beauty—not the farm girl from Grabtown, N.C." (She liked to call Boon Hill "Grabtown," obviously alluding to its macho insensibility and the well-known male habit of "groping" the female anatomy.) "The trouble was," she went on, "I became a victim of my own Hollywood image. Because I was promoted as a sort of siren and played all those sexy broads, people made the mistake of thinking I was like that off the screen."

A short pause.

"They couldn't have been more wrong. There was nothing sophisticated about me. Although no one believes me, I've always been a country girl and I still have a country girl's values." The men in her life never really understood. "No one wanted to know the real me. They preferred the myths."

Frank Sinatra was a myth, too. Perhaps each married a myth, with the result that the marriage became nothing more than another myth—a myth wrapped around two separate myths and fated to go where all myths go when people substitute them for reality: up in smoke.

Their marriage suffered from another very real psychological and emotional problem. Ava was on her way up. Frank was not. His professional life was a shambles. After wrapping up a forgettable movie called *Meet Danny Wilson* (1952), he even began feuding with Mitch Miller, the Artists and Repertoire chief of Columbia Records.

Miller, completely unimpressed by the Sinatra name and charm, began assigning cutesy-pie novelty numbers to him. The worst of these was a duet with a big-bosomed blond star named Dagmar. Its title was "Mama Will Bark." Besides the duet, unbelievable enough on its own, the record included "imitations by Donald Bain." The imitations were presumably of dog barks. And there were more like it: the forgettable "Mairzy Doats," for one.

"No!" Sinatra would cry out. "I won't do any of this shit! It's the worst kind of crap."

When both Columbia and M.C.A. finally dropped him, these two rejections, happening as they did almost back to back, were murder on the Sinatra ego. He especially could not understand why M.C.A. had let him go.

"They never even had to promote me!" he said later. Sinatra blamed it all on Miller. But Miller removed himself from blame for Sinatra's fall: "Columbia Records had advanced him $150,000 to pay his taxes, and it was my job to record songs that were profitable so Columbia could get its money back. I would not select unpromising material deliberately. I would be defeating my own purpose."

Later, after Sinatra had signed on with Capitol

Records and begun to regain his old "magic," Mitch Miller ran into him in Las Vegas. According to the story, Miller put his hand out to Sinatra and said something about letting "bygones be bygones."

"Fuck you!" snapped Frank. "Keep walking."

So Frank was down, and Ava was up. MGM loaned Ava out to Twentieth Century–Fox to producer Darryl F. Zanuck for a screen version of Ernest Hemingway's *The Snows of Kilimanjaro*—a picture always referred to by Hemingway as *The Snows of Zanuck*.

Zanuck had remembered Ava from another Hemingway adaptation—*The Killers*—in which she had played the female lead in the proper smoldering film-noir manner. She was now to play Cynthia, the coarse-grained, outgoing, but battered Hemingway temptress. Sinatra was annoyed that his wife could continue in films without respite—particularly since he was scheduled for a run at the New York Paramount and wanted his wife at his side.

The shooting schedule was trimmed tightly so that Ava's work would be confined to ten days; at the end of that time, she could then accompany her husband to Manhattan. Nevertheless, right at the end, she was forced to stay one extra day.

Ava was enraged—at the studio for extending her shooting schedule, *and* at Frank for what he might do when he learned she would be late. "That motherfucker is going to give me hell when I tell him!" she complained to director Henry King. "And I'm just going to sit there and take it."

And of course, it all happened exactly as she had anticipated.

Their marriage, then, was not off to any particularly great start. Once his stint in New York was finished, Sinatra decided that he and Ava needed a vacation to Hawaii. It was only a temporary respite. Once they were back in the States, the fights began to escalate once again. Newspaper gossips tagged them as the Battling Sinatras, and filled columns of type describing their encounters.

At an Italian restaurant in Los Angeles one night, the owner joined Sinatra at their table for a chat with Frank. For a couple of hours Ava listened in bored silence to talk about baseball, fights, and sports ad nauseam.

Suddenly she stood up and walked out. Sinatra figured she had gone to the ladies' room.

However, when he was finally ready to go home, he couldn't find her at all. She wasn't in the ladies' room, or in the car, or anywhere. In fact, when he got home, he found she wasn't there either. Two days later he got a phone call from Italy. It was Ava. She told him she had driven from the restaurant to Los Angeles International Airport and had taken the first flight out for Rome.

Later they battled about Sinatra's visits to his ex-wife and his children. They battled about Ava'a career. They battled about Ava's continued interest in Artie Shaw. In Rooney. In Mitchum. In everybody.

After the premiere in New York of *The Snows of Kilimanjaro*, Sinatra took her to Bill Miller's Riviera Club in Fort Lee, New Jersey, where he was performing. Ava was happy to see him at work, and to see the appreciative stares of the people in the crowd, saluting *her* for her work in *Kilimanjaro*.

Until she saw Marilyn Maxwell sitting in the front row, beaming up at Frank on the stage.

And then—Christ!—Frank sang "All of Me"—and to Ava it seemed that he was singing it directly to this busty friend of his from the past! She stalked out of the club uttering her usual stream of colorful obscenities, and flew back to Hollywood. Once there she put her wedding ring in an envelope and mailed the damned thing to Sinatra in New York. A dejected Sinatra played a few weeks in St. Louis and finally returned to the Coast, where he drove Ava to the bullfights in Tijuana in an effort to stroke her ruffled feathers.

It was peace, but not for long. Lana Turner, an old friend of both Frank and Ava, was having her own troubles with her current escort, Lex Barker. Barker played Tarzan on the screen, and brought it home with him sometimes. Lana's manager sought help from Sinatra, asking him for a place where his client could get away from her current flame and her rather upset studio. Sinatra agreed to let Lana stay in the house at Palm Springs.

Suddenly, on an otherwise peaceful desert morning, Ava drove up in her car, got out, and with Bappie, entered the house—stunned to find Lana Turner there. "What the hell are you doing here?" she flared up. It was obvious what she thought— that Frank was bedding her down on the side.

"Frank lent me the place." Lana was cool and correct.

As this tableau lengthened, in silent freeze-frame, another car drove up outside, with Frank himself leaping out, obviously in hot pursuit of his fleeing wife. Now Ava was playing the aggrieved wife as well as the pursued lover. A shocked Lana watched as Frank grabbed her roughly and shoved her into a room and locked the door. Bappie was hovering in the background.

Lana and her manager drove to a nearby hotel. Later, when she returned to pick up her clothes, she came upon a melodramatic scene outside the big house. Neighbors milled around, cops stood by police cars parked haphazardly, lights swirled and blinked. At the center of this cluttered scene Francis Albert Sinatra and Ava Gardner Rooney Shaw Sinatra were wrestling and hitting one another in a very realistic imitation of a duel to the death.

Lana ran up screeching, "Cut that out, Frank!" She dove in between the two sluggers. With her manager's help—and with the aid of Bappie and an amused policeman—the couple were finally separated.

Ava fled the scene, hiding out with friends. Sinatra packed up his things and moved out of the house. He bunked in with Jimmy Van Heusen, his songwriting confrère.

What brought Ava and Frank together again was—oddly enough—Governor Adlai Stevenson. He was running for president in the 1952 election. Ava and Frank had promised to appear at a Stevenson rally in Los Angeles. And so, at the Hollywood Palladium, there they were, standing arm in arm and hugging and kissing and adoring one another for the cameras and for the public and for the Democrats.

"I can't do anything myself," Ava cooed, "but I can introduce a wonderful, wonderful man. I'm a great fan of his myself. Ladies and gentlemen, my husband, Frank Sinatra!"

Sidney Skolsky, the columnist, wrote: "They have Stevenson in common." To which Earl Wilson commented: "Politics makes strange bedfellows."

Whatever truce it might be was short-lived. What broke it up this time was Stewart Granger, a friend of Ava's. But it wasn't a love match. It was a career match.

Granger had just finished filming *King Solomon's*

Mines in Kenya and wanted to do another African film to sustain the he-man image he had just acquired. He suggested a remake of Clark Gable's early hit with Jean Harlow, *Red Dust*. He wanted Ava for the character played by Harlow, with Grace Kelley as the icy English "lie-dee."

But then MGM double-crossed Granger when Gable himself asked for the role; Gable's own popularity was slumping at the time and he needed a hit every bit as much as Granger did. Ava was unhappy; she was friendly with Granger and liked him. And she knew Frank would hit the roof if she was bunked in the jungles of Kenya alone with the "king" himself for a couple of months.

But Frank was wrestling with his own demons and paid little attention to the situation—at least, for the moment. He was in deep trouble with the Internal Revenue Service, owing over $100,000 in back taxes. Moreover, he had no gigs at the moment—no movies, no recording dates, no nightclub engagements. He saw nothing ahead and only futility in trying to keep going at all. He was broke. Ava was bringing in all the money.

But there was one ray of sunshine in the darkness. He had read James Jones's book *From Here to Eternity* and had fallen in love with the role of Private Angelo Maggio. He knew it was going to be made into a film. "I know Maggio," he said. "I went to high school with him in Hoboken. I was beaten up with him. I might have been Maggio."

But when push came to shove, he knew he had to hang on to Ava—who suddenly announced that she was going to appear in this *Mogambo* remake of *Red Dust*, to be shot on four-month location in Africa. Humiliation and depression fought each other inside him, tearing him apart. His wife was in one of the year's biggest-budgeted movies. He was unable to get work at all. They were continually scrapping.

On Ava's part, it was no better. She was exhausted from her haggles with MGM about her contract and about her film career. Besides, she thought seriously that she might be pregnant; she had not told Frank. And it was a very bad time in her professional career to be pregnant—facing a four-month ordeal on the Dark Continent.

In the end Frank made up his mind. He was determined to accompany his wife to Africa, to be at her side all during the long schedule. Making the picture would be a grueling chore.

The less said about Africa, the better. Through the first few weeks, Sinatra brooded in the confines of the camp, waiting for Ava to come back from location, and simultaneously waiting for some word from Columbia about *From Here to Eternity*. He was jealous of Gable, of course—but he needn't have been. Gable found Grace Kelly more to his liking than Ava—although he treated them both with little more than fondness. Ava was annoyed at Gable's disinterest, but couldn't help being glad of it as well because it kept Frank off her back.

The Sinatras' wedding anniversary fell during the shooting of the picture. The Battling Sinatras had been married a full year! And it was for this event that Frank produced a surprise show for the production unit, using fifty African singers and dancers as his own "cast of thousands." It was a welcome respite from the hot and humid work.

Shortly after that, Frank got word that he was to

return to shoot a screen test for the part of Maggio. So he flew excitedly to Hollywood.

On November 22, some few days later, Ava flew secretly to London. There she was met by Bappie. She was very sick. At Chelsea Hospital for Women she suffered a miscarriage, which was reported by the press as "a severe case of anemia." She had been right. She *was* pregnant.

"All my life I wanted a baby," Ava said, "and the news that I had lost him (I was sure it was a boy) was the cruelest blow I ever received." About her husband, who wasn't there, she said: "Even though my marriage to Frank was getting shakier every day, I didn't care. I wanted a baby by him."

Frank was back on location in Nairobi by Christmas. On that day—it was Ava's birthday—they celebrated the holidays and Ava's birthday. In spite of their differences, they were show-biz people on that night, and so they projected the entertaining and charming images expected of them.

John Ford, the picture's director, introduced Ava to the district commissioner, the senior British officer in the area, who, along with his wife, was present at the party.

"Ava," Ford joked, "why don't you tell the commissioner what you see in that hundred-and-twenty-pound runt you're married to."

"Well," said Ava with a bland, innocent look, "there's only ten pounds of Frank, but there's a hundred and ten pounds of cock."

Ford almost collapsed. But the commissioner and his wife burst into hearty British laughter.

A few days later a wire arrived for Frank. He had gotten the part! He was to play Maggio in *From Here to Eternity*. He was to report to Hawaii where shooting would commence almost immediately. For the next few months there was almost no communication between him and Ava. But in the spring they were reunited in London, where Ava was making another picture—this time *Knights of the Round Table* opposite Robert Taylor. There she ran into her old friends the Stewart Grangers. Sinatra managed to get a few engagements at London clubs and joined her there.

They fought and they loved. It was just like old times. At one point, he was singing in a nightclub and Ava was watching with Stewart Granger and his wife Jean Simmons. Ava suddenly burst into tears. "Look at that goddamned son of a bitch!" she sobbed. "How can you resist him?"

Then Sinatra got a summons from the studio to appear in New York for the premiere of *From Here to Eternity*. Ava wanted to go with him. She told Frank she would try to get a release from the studio. It took time, but she managed it. When she rushed back to the apartment, she found that Frank had already packed and was waiting for a limo to take him to Heathrow. He hadn't even bothered to wait for her!

Ava blew her top. He blew his top. They parted in wrath, fur flying and tempers blazing.

He went. She stayed.

Then, trying to make a reconciliation by telephone between New York and London, Ava began to sob again. Frank was angry. He couldn't hold it in. "I don't like crying women!" he screamed. And hung up.

Ava sulked. She flew to Spain to stay with some American friends. There she met Luis Miguel Dominguin, almost an institution in Spain. He was the Numero Uno matador of Spain, with a fantastic record of kills. He certainly outclassed her old co-star, Mario Cabre. Not only that, he was a smooth-looking, handsome, muscular guy. At the time he and Ava met, he was in a depressed state. He had been badly gored in the stomach in a recent fight, and was being forced to recuperate for at least a year.

To Ava, Dominguin was the opposite of Sinatra. He was lovable, he was silken, he was affectionate. There were plenty of temptations for Ava, but in the end she decided to fly to the States to see her husband. After all, she *was* married to him.

In New York, there was no Frank out at the airport to greet her, although he was working in town. Of course, Ava had not *told* him she was coming in. Did she expect him to know by ESP? On Frank's side, he suddenly read in the papers one morning that Ava was in town and was staying at the Hampshire House. Why hadn't she come to see him sing?

Well, the hell with him/her!

They ignored one another. At the Sinatra opening at Bill Miller's Riviera in New Jersey, Ava was conspicuous by her absence. Now Dolly, Frank's mother, got into the act. She had a heart-to-heart with Ava at the Hampshire House. She was fond of Ava—for her honesty, her toughness, and her plain-spoken manner. The two of them telephoned Frank.

All three had dinner at Dolly's. Shortly after that, Frank moved out of the Waldorf into the Hampshire House with Ava. Things went better for a time.

Then Ava got the lead role in *The Barefoot Contessa*. That meant a trip to Italy, where the picture was being made at Cinecittà Studios. It was no fun for Ava, even though it might well have been. The conflict had to do with the personalities of the actors with whom she was playing. Mostly it was Rossano Brazzi and Humphrey Bogart.

Rossano Brazzi was a total egotist, a Narcissus, and a complainer. Humphrey Bogart was annoyed at Ava and her relationship with Sinatra, who was a particular friend of Bogey's.

"I'll never figure you broads out," Bogart rasped at her the first time they met on the set. "Half the world's female population would throw themselves at Frank's feet, and here you are flouncing around with guys who wear capes and little ballerina slippers."

Ava knew he was referring to Dominguin. She evaded the issue.

Bappie, a seamstress, a couple of makeup people, a young man who carried stacks of flamenco and Sinatra records, and one of the Fontana sisters had accompanied Ava to Italy for the filming. When they showed up, Bogart made a face at them and turned to Ava. "Let me get a running start toward the set. I don't want to get trampled by your entourage. And if I waited until it passed, I wouldn't get there until Thursday." He kidded her about being a "Boon Hill gypsy," and taunted her about being afraid to drink too much because her Southern accent might reappear and undo her.

For the Christmas holidays, Ava flew to Madrid to get away from the set and her antagonists there. She preferred to be with Dominguin and his cape and little ballerina slippers. The story went that she was in Spain "for the holidays." Frank flew in from New York to be with her in Madrid—"for the holidays."

The reunion turned into something straight out of a bedroom farce. Ava would meet with Dominguin after setting a false trail for Frank. Frank would be looking for her in the wrong places because he had been set up by Ava's seamstress, or her makeup artist, or the guy with the stacks of flamenco and Sinatra records.

All there principals were at the Christmas party. Dominguin looked right through Sinatra, as if he didn't exist. Sinatra fiddled with his cocktail glass and kept drinking. Ava was serenely unaware of any tension and kept up her usual flow of gossip and four-letter words.

Frank flew to New York. Ava flew to Rome. When the film was wrapped, she went back to Spain, where she met Ernest Hemingway. They talked about the Sinatra marriage, which was now in total shambles. To Hemingway, she explained her liaison with Dominguin. "We've been together for two months now, but I speak no Spanish and he speaks no English, so we haven't been able to communicate yet."

"Don't worry," said Hemingway. "You've communicated what counts."

Now came the big news. Sinatra was up for an Academy Award for the role of Maggio. Would he win? Ava didn't seem to care. She didn't even go to the Acadamy Awards ceremony. In fact, not many people knew where she actually was. But of course Sinatra was there—with his daughter, Nancy, Jr., and his son, Frank, Jr. When Frank won, he kissed his daughter, squeezed his son's hand, and went up to claim his Oscar.

Where the hell was Mrs. Sinatra?

Ava was actually not near, but, indeed, neither was she very far away. In the first months of 1954, having finished shooting in Italy, Ava had flown back to the United States. She rented a cottage on the shores of Lake Tahoe. There she was accompanied by her sister Bappie, her corgi Rags, and a house guest.

The house guest was none other than the gored bullfighter Luis Miguel Dominguin. It was Earl Wilson and his wife who tracked her down at a place called Cave Rock, in the neighborhood of Mount Rose. And it was from there that Ava Gardner filed for divorce from Frank Sinatra in the Nevada courts.

In what Wilson called the "divorce" cottage, he, with his wife, was introduced to the ailing bullfighter. Dominguin kissed Mrs. Wilson's hand and smiled happily at the columnist. "Miguel's only staying a couple of days," Ava said airily. "He's going to the Philippines and then to South America, where he has business." She waved Dominguin out for a drink. "Get a piece of ice," she instructed him. "A piece of *ice,*" she repeated, saying the word carefully. "That's not the same as a piece of *ass.*"

With a toss of the shoulder, she told the Wilsons: "He's trying to learn English."

Not a word was mentioned about Frank Sinatra. Her husband.

Dominguin left on schedule. Ava stayed around a bit longer at the lake, and then she was visited by an old friend in an airplane: Howard Hughes. With Hughes she flew away to some undisclosed destination.

Shortly after that she appeared in South America, where she was involved in a four-country publicity tour for *The Barefoot Contessa.* Oddly enough, she rejoined Dominguin there; he was "on business," as she had told Wilson. Dominguin then accompanied her back to New York after she had made a side visit to see Ernest Hemingway in Cuba.

But the affair with Dominguin faded as the bullfighter began regaining his strength and working out for his comeback. Soon Ava was running around with an Italian comedian named Walter Chiari, who just happened to bear a startling physical resemblance to Frank Sinatra, another Italian.

It was definitely all over between the Battling Sinatras.

And yet . . .

In the years that followed, the two of them continued to see each other from time to time—with the circumstances of their reunions a great deal happier than during the time they were married.

It was, if nothing else, a "marriage of inconvenience."

★ 7 ★

The Pack Rats

Humphrey Bogart was one of those rare Hollywood personalities—a star who had stature and clout but was without affectation and pretense. Like Frank Sinatra—and Ava Gardner—he was also one who could use four-letter words whenever they seemed to be the proper words to express his ideas. Since his ideas tended to be of a certain no-nonsense nature, he was known to use a great number of such words. And he had always had a natural aversion to the stodgy Establishment manner of the motion-picture "family."

Sinatra had met Bogart in his early years in Hollywood, and when Frank was on the skids, Bogart had not deserted him like most of his fair-weather friends.

When the still-married Nancy and Frank Sinatra bought a quarter-million-dollar house in Holmby Hills, an expensive and exclusive part of Beverly Hills, both of them formed a fast friendship with the Bogarts—Mrs. Bogart was Lauren Bacall. When Nancy kept the house as part of the divorce settlement, Frank continued to visit her and the children there, and also to drop in on Bogey and Bacall.

And, anyway, Frank had always been a part of the Holmby Hills Rat Pack, named casually by Betty Bacall one day. This "Pack" was an unofficial organization that did not really exist at all, according to those who were members of it and should know. Actually, the Rat Pack was Bogart's way of thumbing his nose at the big shots and half asses who ran the motion-picture industry. The actor's independence usually become slightly abrasive when he wanted to show real contempt for someone or something that irked him.

And he could always call on plenty of help when he needed it.

Bogart's first words when someone came in to see him usually were: "Let's have a drink." But his second thoughts went something like this: "Okay. Now who can we louse up today? Let's get started." *That* was the purpose of the nonpurpose organization: to louse up the stuffed shirts and kick mud in the faces of the high and mighty.

In the early days of the Pack, Judy Garland was vice-president and Bacall was den mother. David Niven, another independent spirit, was an officer of the Pack. In fact, every member was an officer of one kind or another—with the responsibilities and titles shifting from day to day. Jimmy Van Heusen, the song writer, and a fast friend of Sinatra, was an officer, and so was Irving "Swifty" Lazar, the high-powered agent; actually, he had so much money he was automatically dubbed treasurer by Bogart.

John Huston was a Rat in good standing. To be in good standing meant that you had to do something ratty that ran against the Hollywood grain. Huston's big act of defiance occurred in the 1950s when he began to shoot films in foreign countries, far from the influence and pressure of the studio brass. Bogart thought that was splendid ratsmanship. "John's got real guts. He never lets them tell him what to do. If somebody comes to him and asks him to do a picture, he'll say, 'Fine—but we've got to make it in Tanganyika.' He's one of the few real *souls* around this crummy place."

As for eligibility in the Rat Pack, Bogart was always somewhat mysterious about that. "We always know a rat when we see one," he insisted. Usually it was anyone who liked to stay up late at night and drink quantities of liquor. Night people were always good Rat Packers.

When *Life* magazine interviewed the Bogarts about the Pack, Betty Bacall said, "We really *stood* for something. We had *officers* . . . we had principles. You *had* to stay up late and get drunk." And then she added, as if it made all the sense in the world: "All our members were against the P.T.A." And so for outsiders who were against the Pack: "Anybody who attacked one of our members . . . We *got* them."

Initially Bogart did most of the hazing. A new member might not know anything about the Pack. He might be there simply to be scrutinized by Bogart. And the hazing would resemble college fraternity rites. Bogart would aim deadly insults at the prospect, with a straight face, and with no indication that there was any intention in his thrusts. Once "in," a member would know how solidly he or she was in the group by the way Bogart talked. Here's what Bogart had to say about two of his favorites.

"John Huston looks like an ape when he's bored. Harry Warner was giving a bunch of guys a lecture on the international market one day. It was one of the dullest speeches I ever heard in my life. Huston was pretending to listen, but as the Great Man kept talking away, Huston's face gradually began to look just like an ape's. I felt like handing him a banana."

As for Frank Sinatra: "The thing about him is, he's a cop hater. If you ask him a question, any question, he thinks you're a cop." He went on. "I think Betty and I must be parent substitutes for him, or something. He's always around here." At another time, he spoke this way: "The trouble with Sinatra is that he thinks heaven is a place where there are all broads and no newspapermen. He doesn't know he'd be better off if it were the other way around."

Sinatra was the quintessential Rat Packer in his aggressive indifference to what moviegoers expected of stars and what Hollywood expected of its citizens.

By 1956, it seemed as though almost anybody who dropped in to Bogart's place became an automatic member of the Rat Pack. Judy Garland's husband, Sid Luft, the actor Paul Douglas, the comic Joey Bishop, and many others. The members sometimes assembled on Bogart's yacht *Santana*.

This was the period when Bogart was dying of cancer. He was blunt about it, let everyone know. "Nothing to be ashamed of like some other diseases I could have had. Why not talk about it?"

But the end was near. He died on January 14, 1957. Sinatra heard about it at the Copacabana where he was performing, and was almost too sick to go on. In fact, he canceled two appearances.

John Huston delivered the eulogy. He was eloquent about Betty Bacall. "She was gallant; she knew death was there every hour of the day and night. And out of the power of her love she was able

Young Frank Sinatra (*right*), one of The Hoboken Four, pictured with host Major Bowes on the 1935 *Amateur Hour.*

Fans mob Sinatra in Pasadena, California, on his way in 1943 to make the movie *Higher and Higher.*
(AP/WIDE WORLD PHOTOS)

Crowds jam the sidewalk to see Frank Sinatra appear in person at the New York Paramount in wartime (1944).
(AP/WIDE WORLD PHOTOS)

Sinatra and Phil Silvers, in USO uniforms, ready to enter-
tain troops overseas during World War II.

Sinatra being fingerprinted
for a gun permit (1947).
He said he often stayed out
late at night and wanted
the gun for protection.
(AP/WIDE WORLD PHOTOS)

With his wife, Nancy Sinatra,
leaving a Hollywood
night-club in 1946.
(AP/WIDE WORLD PHOTOS)

Frank Sinatra and actress
Ava Gardner at their marriage
in Philadelphia in 1951.

The accuser (Lee Mortimer)
watches the accused (Frank
Sinatra) in a Beverly Hills
courthouse after an
altercation in a Sunset
Strip nightclub (1947).

Sinatra, as Maggio in *From Here to Eternity,* poses with
fellow actors Montgomery Clift and Burt Lancaster.

Giving testimony before a California state legislature committee regarding 1957 "wrong-door raid" on apartment mistaken for that of Marilyn Monroe's friend.

October, 1957: Sinatra and Lauren Bacall at the Hollywood premiere of *Pal Joey*.
(AP/WIDE WORLD PHOTOS)

Right: With Tommy Dorsey at a 1956 stage show, years after his original appearance with the bandleader.
(AP/WIDE WORLD PHOTOS)

"The Clan", circa 1960: Frank Sinatra, Dean Martin, Peter Lawford, Joey Bishop, and Sammy Davis, Jr.

Arriving at his fiftieth birthday party in Beverly Hills with his two daughters, Tina, left, and Nancy, right (1965).

Entertainers Frank Sinatra
and Frank Sinatra, Jr.
greet each other during
a break as both appear
at different Las Vegas hotels
in 1966.

With Mia Farrow:
Sinatra on the town in
Miami (January, 1967).

Escorting Jacqueline Kennedy Onassis at the 21 Club in
New York in September, 1975, just after a concert at the
Uris Theater.

Frank Sinatra and his mother, Dolly, in Palm Springs at the dedication in 1971 of the medical facility named for his father; with Vice President Spiro Agnew, Nancy Reagan, and Governor Ronald Reagan. (AP/WIDE WORLD PHOTOS)

Sinatra flanked in 1976 by Gregory DePalma, Thomas Marson, Carlo Gambino, Jimmy Fratianno, and, in front, Richard Fusco. The U.S. Attorney's office has blocked out one figure. (AP/WIDE WORLD PHOTOS)

With wife, Barbara Marx Sinatra, leaving the wedding of Gerald Ford's daughter, Susan, and Charles Vance in Palm Desert, 1979.

Sinatra and the Peter Duchin orchestra perform at the gala Carnegie Hall reopening in December, 1986.

to hide her grief and go on being her own familiar self for Bogey—a flawless performance."

Sinatra, because he was unmarried, was free to escort Betty Bacall in public for at least a year after Bogart's death. At one point it was rumored that they were engaged.

She had always liked him, and had found him one of the most entertaining of her husband's many guests. She particularly liked the sign he was said to have had hanging in his room at home: "Nobody knows the trouble I've seen. And believe me, *nobody cares*."

She knew him better than many of his contemporaries. "When he's with you," she told a magazine writer, "he adores you. He's charming and witty and fun. And he's a wonderful person to have as a friend. . . . But that boyish quality fools you. Frank's strong, don't think he isn't. You may get the idea that he wants to lean on you, but actually he wants to be boss."

When he was being his own obnoxious self, he annoyed her. At a party one night he was working over someone during one of his typical *enfant terrible* rages, and he turned to find Bacall watching him.

"What are you staring at me for?" he yelled at her.

"Listen, Frank," she said, flaring up. "I'm not *staring*. I'm only using my two eyes."

"Yeah?" Sinatra responded, now furious. "Well, any dame with class uses *three*!"

There was a short silence, and then, as both of them realized the absurdity of the remark, they burst into hysterical merriment.

The two of them were seen frequently in public at the Villa Capri, where they always sat at Sinatra's special booth. Sinatra also dined there with Gloria Vanderbilt, a young starlet named Joan Blackman, and Marlene Dietrich. It was widely whispered that Sinatra was still carrying the torch for Ava, and so no serious intentions were suspected.

But when Frank traveled to Nice for location shooting for his new picture, *Kings Go Forth* (1958), the cat leaped out of the bag. Actually it was an English columnist working for the London *Evening Express* who broke the story in September, 1957, that Sinatra and Betty Bacall would marry in six months' time—"barring an act of Providence or Ava Gardner." The columnist wrote: "I understand Sinatra is anxious to keep his marriage plans a secret and that he will probably deny it, but you can take his denials with a pinch of salt."

Now everybody began asking each of the principals separately what was up. It was an embarrassing time for both of them. Then, in March 1958, about fourteen months after Bogart's death, Louella Parsons announced that the two of them would marry. The story went that Frank had been overheard at dinner at the Imperial Gardens proposing to her. Betty, according to Parsons, admitted that she had been asked and said she had accepted. Irving Lazar assured Parsons that "they'll marry."

They did not. They went their separate ways. In fact, Walter Winchell had dinner with Sinatra at the time—Sinatra was working in Miami—and wrote: "Frank Sinatra and Lauren Bacall will not be married in the near future or at any time." Sinatra was quoted as saying that he and Betty were "very, very dear friends." And that was it.

Betty Bacall tried to keep her sense of humor

over the situation, but it was difficult, considering all the gossip. She later married Jason Robards, Jr.

Tony Curtis understood Frank better than many other people who knew him did. A member of the Rat Pack in good standing, Curtis analyzed the situation this way: "Frank always does this when the husband of one of his friends dies. Doris Vidor, when Charles died. Mrs. Buddy Adler, when her husband died. He called up and said, 'Anything I can do?' Sometimes some women mistook his consideration and thought he was in love. Listen, this is one of the most decent men I've ever met. He's one of the biggest prudes I've ever met. He's an old-fashioned man. I've never heard him use a vulgar word in front of a woman. And maybe, when he called them up, some women got the wrong idea. They thought that he was interested in them as prospects for marriage. You know women. They're always thinking of marriage."

Already Frank had been getting back into the swing of things, slugging it out with the media. In May 1957 he sued *Look* magazine for $2,300,000 for a three-part profile written about him by Bill Davidson, a writer with whom he had always managed good personal relations. "I have always maintained that any writer or publication has a right to discuss or criticize my professional activities as a singer or actor," Sinatra said. "But I feel an entertainer's right to privacy should be just as inviolate as any other person's right to privacy."

One of the anecdotes that Sinatra rejected as untrue was based on an incident that supposedly took place at the 1956 Democratic Convention, where Sinatra had sung the National Anthem. An elderly gentleman was said to have put his hand on Sinatra's arm as he was leaving the platform, and inquired politely: "Aren't you going to sing 'The Yellow Rose of Texas,' Frank?"

Davidson's story said that Frank replied: "Take the hand off the suit, creep!"

And the elderly gentleman turned out to be Speaker Sam Rayburn of the U.S. House of Representatives.

Although Rayburn himself denied the incident, there were more items involved in the suit. The second installment, titled "Why Sinatra Hates the Press," revolved around Davidson's theory that Sinatra had suffered emotional scars in his childhood through his mother's neglect; he compensated for this trauma through fantasies about his youth. Because memories of the press could expose his illusions, Sinatra "hated" and feared them—and, for that reason, fought them.

The suit never came to trial. On February 8, 1963—almost six years later—Sinatra's attorneys filed to have it dismissed.

Sinatra was now concentrating his activities on two phases of the entertainment business: motion pictures and records. After *Eternity* he had begun to get meaty parts in dramatic films. The list was impressive: *Suddenly* (1954); *Not as a Stranger* (1955); *The Man with the Golden Arm* (1955); *The Pride and the Passion* (1957); *The Manchurian Candidate* (1962). There were also comedies: *The Tender Trap* (1955); *A Hole in the Head* (1959); *Come Blow your Horn* (1963). And musicals: *Guys and Dolls* (1955); *High Society* (1956); *Pal Joey* (1957); *Can-Can* (1960). And there were the showbiz jobs: *Ocean's Eleven* (1960); *Sergeants Three*

(1962); *Four for Texas* (1963); *Robin and the Seven Hoods* (1964).

An interesting pattern emerges from this list. Sinatra was devoting most of his talent to moviemaking during the decade directly following his astonishing success in *From Here to Eternity*. As a result of that success and his Oscar-winning performance, he was cast in a number of interesting pictures playing roles in which he could show his abilities and increase his range. In between, of course, he did the musicals; he was still in the business of music and he had staged a comeback with his records.

Then there were the "show-biz" jobs—the comedies that were mostly send-ups or parodies. What seemed to be happening was that while Sinatra was extending his dramatic range, he was internally individualizing himself—creating a new personal role, perhaps. Sinatra's personal life seemed to be becoming his professional life as well. He was as anxious to promote his own image as he was to make good pictures.

The casting in the pictures was the tip-off. Beginning with *Ocean's Eleven*, more and more of Sinatra's personal "pals"—in some cases actual members of Bogart's old Rat Pack—began appearing with him. That cast included Dean Martin, Sammy Davis, Jr., Peter Lawford, and Joey Bishop. All four of these appeared again in *Sergeants Three*. *Robin and the Seven Hoods* had Dean Martin, Sammy Davis, Jr., and Peter Falk. By that time Peter Lawford was—well . . .

The image Sinatra created was certainly based on the man/myth image that Bogart exhibited in his later years: the rough, tough, heart-of-gold, nice guy alienated from society. One friend put it this way about Bogart: "His basset-hound look is part of his basic appeal. Put in its cultural perspective, it makes him the all-American underdog." Another thought about Bogart: "His hardness is superficial. Underneath he is good. The basic values are there."

Whether or not he sought deliberately to pattern himself after Bogart, somehow Sinatra managed to fuse these basic qualities into his own persona. The Bogart–Sinatra independence, the Bogart–Sinatra obsession with spitting in the eye of the Establishment, the to-hell-with-it attitude toward the press— all these elements emerged after the sensational comeback of the early 1950s.

That Sinatra saw himself as something of a Bogart was quite evident in a statement he made about Bogart's acting abilities and the quality of the characters he was able to portray. "There'll never be another performer like Bogey was," he said. The characters he played, Sinatra noted, always "had a lot of fun" and enjoyed life. "They had cynicism, and they had honesty, and he was a seedy character, but he had honor all the time." And he was a perfectionist, exactly like Sinatra.

There seemed to be no argument that in the 1950s Frank Sinatra reached the peak of his artistry in the recording business, too. In spite of the contemporary interest in the loud shouters and in the amplified groups, Sinatra was able to compete with them in some of his best "revivals" of early-1930s pop classics. Several of his Capitol albums—*Songs for Swingin' Lovers, A Swingin' Affair,* and *Come Fly with Me*—are generally conceded to be his best.

Competing with the "new" music, Sinatra's concert-style presentations sold heavily and well.

Actually, it was the development of the LP disc, which had been introduced in 1948, that led to the "concert" style of showcasing songs. In Sinatra's instance, this concert-style became even more. Each album had a theme, or strong basic idea, to it. In the music world, this type of album came to be called the "concept" album. From 1957 to 1966, Sinatra had no top singles, but he had twenty-seven albums that ranked in *Billboard*'s top ten! His 1958 album *Only the Lonely* stayed on the charts for 120 weeks.

Maturity and life experiences had changed his voice, deepening it and darkening it, making the mellowness of his early records into something coarser. His ability to dramatize himself now—probably because of his hard dramatic work in his best movies—gave his words a much more emotional quality.

And his ballad singing style had improved, too. He was now able to interpret the words and mood of any original song writer in terms of the Sinatra personality. His own emotional problems, publicized in his encounters and romances with many different women, tended to give his image a dynamic and glamorous cast.

The lyrics, heard by the now-middle-aged bobby-soxers who had seen him at the Paramount, now inspired visions of Ava Gardner and the tempestuous affair and marriage they had lived through. He was making a personal statement about his own life-style, and making it in his unique way to those young women who had listened to him and squealed for him in the early days of his career. As John

Rockwell wrote in *Sinatra: An American Classic:* "The best of them, and Sinatra is the very best of all, project a personality that infuses their work, transforming songs by others into the most immediate of individual statements."

And what of Sinatra's personal life—over and above the women he was seen out with and rumored to be having affairs with?

He was, in fact, out-Bogarting Bogart. Bogart had once dubbed him president of the Rat Pack. Now he seemed to be becoming more than just president. And the Rat Pack was taking on new energy and new parameters. First of all, Sinatra chose not to be called "rat" as in the early days. Now the group had a new name. Milton Berle once said: "The first time I ever heard about the Clan was when I read about it in *Life*." At that time Berle was a member of the group, and was called its "jester."

Paul O'Neil, a writer for a special issue of *USA Entertainment*, dated December 22, 1958, wrote about the Clan and what it stood for. "Nonconformity is now the key to social importance, and that Angry Middle-Aged Man, Frank Sinatra, is its prophet and reigning social monarch." Everybody in the Clan, according to O'Neil, had to own at least a quarter-million-dollar home, outfit themselves at an expensive haberdashery on Hollywood and Vine, exchange posh gifts, and own or plan to own a Dual Ghia, a luxury Italian car with only one hundred units manufactured each year.

Sinatra snorted about O'Neil's article. "There's no Clan," he told Sidney Skolsky for publication. "How could there be, with Sammy Davis, Jr., a member?" Joe Hyams, another columnist, wrote: "In Hollywood Sinatra lives in a mountain hideout.

His world is called the Clan. It's peopled by other headliners like himself."

By October 1959 all the columnists were writing about the Clan, most claiming that it was an updated version of Bogart's Rat Pack. "To be one of the Clan you have to be kookie," Al Aronowitz noted in the *New York Post*, "and you have to be hip in their way of hip, but you have to have talent." There was an element of economics involved in being a Clan member. The Clan played together, worked together, and made movies together.

The members of the Clan were generally described as a bunch of performers who hung out with Sinatra. Mainly it consisted of Dean Martin, Sammy Davis, Jr., Joey Bishop, Tony Curtis, and Peter Lawford. Martin, of course, had been a star for some years as the straight man to a multi-talented comedian named Jerry Lewis. When the team broke up, it was usually said that Lewis could do anything, but Martin could only sing, and not too well, at that. Davis was an interesting black comic who had converted to Judaism, and who had suffered the loss of one eye in an automobile accident. It was Sinatra's interest in him, and his personal help in bringing Davis back into the business after his injury, that cemented their relationship.

Bishop was an introverted person, who had appeared here and there on television game shows but was not a star of any magnitude until Sinatra pushed him into the limelight. He served eventually as the talk-show host on ABC-TV opposite Johnny Carson. Curtis was of course an excellent comedy actor who had often been miscast in roles in Hollywood epics. He was bright and brash and did not always respect the people of the media—leaving him open to all kinds of criticism and contempt by the journalistic brigade. Peter Lawford was a lightweight actor who had appeared in a number of romantic films just after World War II, but whose main claim to fame was his marriage to Patricia Kennedy, the sister of the two *big* Kennedys—John Fitzgerald and Robert Fitzgerald—and the daughter of old Joe Kennedy.

Sinatra's finger-snapping ebullience, even when he was down, had always impressed Bogart, who now somehow seemed to be the godfather of this outfit. Without really intending it, Frank Sinatra was thus carrying on Bogey's irreverent role and making it work.

A comic at the Copacabana in 1960 more or less characterized the change that had occurred in the image of Frank Sinatra. "I heard it in a little place Frank Sinatra owns called Hollywood," Jackie Kannon said. "Not since the late thirties when Louis B. Mayer ruled from his Metro throne, has anyone had such power," John C. Bowes wrote in an *American Weekly* article. Richard Gehman claimed in *Good Housekeeping* that Sinatra was a powerful "law unto himself," and that he had become "the most feared man in Hollywood."

"While I was in Miami Beach on this story," Gehman related, "my phone rang at four in the morning. Word had apparently been circulated that I was writing an article." The title of the piece, incidentally was "The Disturbing Truth about Sinatra." Anyway, "A low voice said, 'If you know what's good for you, lay off Frank.' The receiver clicked in my ear. At first I was convinced it was a joke. The trouble was, my rapidly beating heart didn't act as if it had been a joke, nor did my shaking hand. It had to be a prank, I reasoned. . . . But I could not help being disturbed."

Gehman's article concluded with these ominous words: "It would be disturbing indeed if this enormous power were in the hands of a completely stable and predictable human being. When it is in the hands of a man torn by emotions that he apparently either cannot or does not care to control, it is something to view with alarm."

But those around Sinatra were not concered about the allegedly "ominous" implications of the Clan. Dean Martin said, "It's silly to call it anything like the Clan or the Group. If anything, it's more like the P.T.A.—a Perfect Togetherness Association." Peter Lawford said, "Now look—that Clan business—I mean, that's hokey. I mean, it makes us sound like children—like we all wore sweat shorts that said, 'The Clan' . . . We're just a lot of people on the same wave length. We like each other. What's wrong with that?" Lawford went on to say that he had been asked about the Clan wherever he went, even France. "This French reporter comes up to me and says, '*Êtes-vous un rat?*' . . . She's asking me about the Rat Pack. But there's no word in French for Rat Pack, you dig?"

You dig was a Clan phrase; of course it was simple Harlem talk that had worked its way into the American slang lexicon during the 1960s. But the Clan had a more specialized vocabulary composed of ordinary slang, street talk, hip musician terms, hoodlum slang, college cant, and even teenage argot.

To the Clan, a good time or a good thing was a "gas"; a great guy or girl was a "gasser." A bungler or "square" to the average American, was a "Harvey." A "bunter" was a "loser," a Clan word that worked itself into the vernacular. "Cool" meant good, attractive, fun, and a variety of other things. "Crazy" meant anything that was "cool."

There were more: A "fink" was a disloyal person, or a jerk. "Clyde" was a code word meaning just about anything; it was used deliberately *not* to specify something obvious to other Clan members. "Charlies" were admirable female breasts. But "Charly," in the singular, was a substitute word for anyone whose name was forgotten. "Sam" meant the same as "Charly." A "quin" was an easy female pickup. "Mother" was the euphemistic version of Harlem's "motherfucker." "Hacked" or "pissed" meant angry. "Pissed" or "smashed" meant drunk. The male genitals, and much of the nearby pelvic areas of the body, were referred to as one's "bird." "Rain" was a washout—like a gathering or a dull party. "Ring-a-ding" meant something exceptional. "Ring-a-ding-ding" meant something more than exceptional. And so on.

Meanings would change from one sentence to another, keeping outsiders baffled and dizzy trying to follow the ebb and flow of the talk. Much of the conversation tended to be inconsequential. The Clan had a habit of "telegraphing" its repartee. Instead of telling each other jokes or anecdotes, they simply communicated by using the punch line of a joke— that joke, of course, had to be an "in" joke of the moment. Thus only the boffo lines of jokes, or cryptic abbreviations of incomprehensible punch lines, sufficed as deep conversation.

An outsider might sit there smiling but wondering what kind of crazy language he was listening to. To make it worse, once one of these truncated boffo lines was uttered, every Clan member present would dissolve into hilarious mirth, slapping their thighs and giggling helplessly.

The Clan was more active than Bogart's Rat Pack. It began to pay visits to nightclubs to throw in digs or gags from the audience. One evening the Clan went to a nightclub to honor one of their buddies, a comic named Sonny King. Leaking news of the impending visit helped to pack the small Slate Brothers club on La Cienega Boulevard in Los Angeles. During the "visit," Dean Martin and Frank Sinatra poured whiskey over the comic and almost became part of the act themselves.

Skolsky wrote later that the evening was a kind of college initiation "to see if Sonny could get into the fraternity known as The Clan." Other members of the audience were not amused.

The Clan visited Eddie Fisher's opening at the Cocoanut Grove in the Ambassador Hotel, one of Wilshire Boulevard's swankiest establishments. In the middle of Eddie Fisher's song, "That Face," Dean Martin yelled out from the audience: "If I were you, I wouldn't be working. I'd be home with her." He was referring to Elizabeth Taylor's near-fatal bout with pneumonia.

Fisher smiled, and some of the audience thought it very funny. There was some more ribbing during Fisher's performance. Then Sinatra, Martin, Sammy Davis, Jr., and Joey Bishop charged onto the stage, liquor glasses in their hands. Peter Lawford remained in his chair. For twenty minutes the group recited dirty limericks, did imitations, and indulged in all kinds of shenanigans.

Hedda Hopper commented: "Frank and his hench-men took over and ruined Eddie's performance."

Variety said that what was presumably meant to be sophisticated humor "came off with a thud. The audience was not amused . . . [by] The Clan's soph-omore pranks." Sidney Skolsky wrote: "You sensed a feeling of audience resentment. . . . This was the first time The Clan played to a hostile audience; the first time they received unfavorable comment in the press."

But Eddie Fisher didn't mind the interruptions at all. "They had called to say they wanted to present me with a box of one hundred fine silk handker-chiefs, and I wasn't sure what to expect. I knew they would heckle me; it had happened a couple of times in Las Vegas, in the spirit of fun, and every-body enjoyed it. But that night, before I had a chance to sing a single note, the Clan walked on stage and took over completely, while I sat on the sidelines, watching them horse around. Then they presented me with the silk handkerchiefs. The box was full of rags.

"I loved it, but the people in that audience had witnessed the antics of the Clan once too often and were impatient for me to get on with the show. They began to hiss and boo until the Clan left the stage and I could begin my act. Elizabeth was very upset; I loved the whole thing, and it turned out to be a great opening night. These men were my friends."

Sinatra said about these nightly visits to night-clubs: "We never hurt anybody and we don't plan to. . . . I've never yet seen an audience dislike what we do. Like for instance the other night . . . what we did to Eddie Fisher. It was beautiful. When we jumped onstage, he broke up and couldn't sing anymore. I never saw a reaction from a crowd like we saw that night—I swear it was like New Year's Eve. . . . What we do is a rib—a good-natured kind of rib. Really, we rib ourselves." Later, at a Copacabana opening, Sammy Davis, Jr., made light of these criticisms: "The Clan? Why, that's just a little group of ordinary guys that get together once a year to take over the entire world."

In a *TV Guide* article Garry Moore was not amused. "Guys like Frank Sinatra and his bunch of parasites . . . think I'm square because I rehearse and observe standards of good taste. Sinatra and Dean Martin and the rest of 'the Clan' are no credit to the business. They think it's clever to pull off-color gags on the air. . . . I'd rather be a cornball than descend to the gutter."

John McLain, a television critic, wrote: "They are certainly liberal to a fault, insanely generous, and public spirited. They are a crazy and wonderful part of America."

David Susskind invited Richard Gehman and Marya Mannes to represent the opposition to Sinatra on one of his shows, with Toots Shor, Lenore Lemmon, Joe E. Lewis, Ernie Kovacs, and Jackie Gleason to discuss the Clan and Sinatra.

Mannes tried to get the comics to go after Sinatra by stating that the Clan lacked decency and gallantry, and dealt in brashness and arrogance. Gleason stood up for Sinatra, saying he was just pretending to project the frivolous image of the times. Most of the other comics simply told jokes from their own files and didn't bother to attack Sinatra.

Susskind finally exclaimed: "Gentlemen, you make him sound like Albert Schweitzer!"

When Sidney Skolsky predicted that the Clan was dissolving, Dorothy Kilgallen wrote: "Reports elsewhere that the Frank Sinatra Clan has disbanded, or is coming apart at the seams, are far from factual. It's still a tightly knit organization, even if some members had to pretend to go 'underground' for obvious reasons."

"Clan, Clan, Clan," Joey Bishop said in one of his stand-up routines. "I'm sick and tired of hearing things about the Clan—just because a few of us guys get together once a week with sheets over our heads!"

Nevertheless, the new image of the middle-aged swinger was a Sinatra invention, and it seemed to be paying off in a business sense for him and for members of the "nonexistent" Clan. It would be some years before that image changed.

In the meantime, Sinatra, in his bachelorhood, had not been resting. He was adding constantly to the seemingly endless list of his sexual affairs and encounters with women in Hollywood and elsewhere.

★ 8 ★

Girls, Girls, Girls

When he had moved out of the Holmby Hills place in the early 1950s after his divorce, Frank Sinatra had purchased a house for himself in Coldwater Canyon. Remembering the ogling neighbors during the first period of his success in New Jersey, when he had often looked out to see others staring in, he installed a sign on the electronically controlled gate to the estate that bluntly read:

> IF YOU HAVEN'T BEEN INVITED, YOU'D BETTER HAVE
> A DAMNED GOOD REASON FOR RINGING THIS BELL!

It wasn't especially that Sinatra didn't *want* people in; it was that he only wanted the people *he* wanted in—and that began to include a very large number of friends and associates, both of the male, and, most especially, the female persuasion.

The place appeared to be designed for pure hedonism. One wall, entirely plate glass, overlooked Hollywood and the Pacific Ocean in the distance. Below this huge window on the world was a flood-lit swimming pool. And in the next room, there was a private screening room. Plus a state-of-the-art stereo system . . . that only played Sinatra records.

But it was as a result of the quiet nights when Sinatra brought home the women he had met that the place gained its reputation. Jule Styne once told of a time when Sinatra, playing the swinging bachelor, got his complicated schedule mixed up after inviting him and at the last minute told Styne not to come: "I've got a date with someone you know," he told him. "She wouldn't want you to know she was here. Go to a hotel for the night."

Styne couldn't help but be intrigued. Who in hell was Sinatra romancing now? Obviously someone the press knew nothing about. Obviously someone important in the world of entertainment. Once ensconced at the hotel, Styne discovered he was unable to go to sleep; he'd left his sleeping pills at Sinatra's place. He cabbed over to Coldwater Canyon, entered the place through a side entrance only the initiated knew about, and glanced inside.

"There was Frank with this girl in his arms on the step," Styne recalled. "There was love-making music—a Sinatra ballad. He was going to take her upstairs. He was reciting poetry to her ... (some awful garbage!) ... I got a good look at her."

Styne started laughing. "It was our manicurist!"

Sinatra's tastes were eclectic. He had interests in all varieties of womanhood. The obscure ... and the famous. For example, he was frequently seen in public with Judy Garland, Carolyn Jones, Natalie Wood, Shirley MacLaine, and Dinah Shore—to mention only a handful.

In the 1950's he had found a retreat where he could go when the Hollywood scene began to pall. He bought a huge three-acre estate in Palm Springs that had once belonged to Al Jolson. There was a guest cottage at the end of a big swimming pool.

Frank would charter an aircraft to take a few of his select friends from L.A. to Palm Springs for the weekend—or just for the evening!

His taste in women constantly changed. Not only manicurists and hatcheck girls—but the biggest stars in the movie firmament. One of the biggest at that time was Marilyn Monroe. Sinatra had dated her a few times, but when she married Joe DiMaggio, he began to visit them at their house or dined out with the two of them. He had known Jolting Joe from the old days when DiMaggio was playing baseball for the New York Yankees and Sinatra was in the early, up phase of his career.

The DiMaggio–Monroe marriage was a stormy one. Monroe was at the height of her fame, eager to make a success with the critics as well as the public, although she had no real training as an actress. DiMaggio had been a star and had been married; he wanted a wife with whom he could settle down and enjoy the money he had made and the fame he had acquired. Sinatra met Monroe in 1954, the same year she married DiMaggio. At the time, she was scheduled to play opposite him in a movie called *Pink Tights*. But then, on January 14, she was married to DiMaggio in the City Hall in San Francisco.

A quarrel arose between the newlyweds—the subject being *Pink Tights. And* Frank Sinatra. DiMaggio wanted his new wife to quit the motion-picture business and settle down with him. The Yankee Clipper also didn't want her to make a picture with Sinatra.

"Joe didn't give me a reason why he didn't want me to do the picture," Marilyn said later. "All he kept saying was that the picture wasn't for me. So I refused to do it. When they asked me why, the only excuse I could give them was that I thought the script was bad."

The truth was that Marilyn *knew* why DiMaggio didn't want her to do *Pink Tights*. "Joe's Italian blood really came to a boil when I told him the studio was putting me into a musical with Frank Sinatra," she said. "That confused me because I always thought they were old friends. That's when I got my first real indication that Joe wasn't for me. He was too damned jealous."

As a result of Monroe's refusal to do the picture, Darryl Zanuck suspended her temporarily from Twentieth Century–Fox. But of course she was eventually reinstated and cast as a singer and dancer in *There's No Business Like Show Business*. The DiMaggios moved from San Francisco, where they lived just after their marriage, and bought a place in Beverly Hills.

And so everything seemed to settle down for the newlyweds. But not for long. In the fall of 1954, Marilyn Monroe was making *The Seven Year Itch* in New York. In one unforgettable scene, the director Billy Wilder arranged to have the wind blow up from a subway grate over which she was standing and hoist her skirts high in the air. They shot the scene over and over, while crowds of people, including a livid DiMaggio, watched.

"That was the living end," as Monroe put it. It was all over at that point. The DiMaggios began battling every time they saw one another. Finally, less than a month later, Monroe filed for an interlocutory decree in the Santa Monica court. The decree was granted on October 27, 1954, ending the marriage just a little over nine months after it had begun.

At this point DiMaggio suddenly made a complete about-face. Now he didn't want the divorce. He wanted her back. But he had a funny way of showing it. Apparently he had decided he wanted to know whom his wife was going out with—and how often. He got in touch with Sinatra again. He was disturbed, he told Sinatra, about his disintegrating relationship with Monroe. He suspected she was having an affair with someone. He wanted to find out who it was and settle it in his own way. Sinatra agreed to help; he would hire a private detective to shadow Marilyn Monroe. The man he got was Barney Ruditsky, an ex–New York cop; Ruditsky, who had no California license to practice, hired a private eye named Phil Irwin to help him. Apparently some of the reports led DiMaggio to believe that his rival was not a man, but a woman!

Later on, Marilyn Monroe figured that it must have been Sinatra who suggested to her ex-husband that his rival might be—well, let's let Monroe tell it her way. "I'm not sure exactly what Frankie told him," Monroe said. "He was lots better friends with Joe then than Frankie was with me. He probably just wanted to tease Joe and figured Joe wouldn't take it too seriously. I think it was something ridiculous—like I was having an affair with this *woman* from the studio. Imagine—a woman!

"They were probably sitting around having a few drinks, and Frankie started to joke around. He liked to joke around a lot, but Joe never did. Joe must have believed whatever Frankie told him."

Monroe was visiting a friend, Sheila Stewart, at an apartment on Waring Avenue in Beverly Hills on the night of November 5, 1954, shortly after her official separation from DiMaggio. At least, that was factually true, if not the whole truth.

What happened next depends on which account you want to believe. One of the most impartial is that of Anthony Summers, a British journalist and former BBC announcer and writer. He got most of his information from the Associated Press newspaperman, James Bacon, based in L.A.

Bacon was at the Villa Capri restaurant that same night. The Villa Capri was not one of the most prestigious of dining halls in the city; it was strictly a rendezvous for the spaghetti-and-meatball set. That night two of its most famous patrons were there—Sinatra and DiMaggio.

Hank Sanicola, Sinatra's manager, was with them. DiMaggio was in a dour mood. It was the week after his separation, and he had heard from Monroe that there was no chance of a reconciliation. Bacon, who saw them from a nearby table, recollected that DiMaggio was in "a terrible mood."

Meanwhile, out on Waring Avenue in Beverly Hills, Phil Irwin, the private eye, was cruising along the street in his car nosing around for whatever he could find. And there, parked not far from the apartment, he saw Monroe's Cadillac at the curb. He immediately contacted Ruditsky by phone and told him the news. Ruditsky rushed to the scene.

After a bit of surveillance, the two detectives compared notes. Leaving Irwin covering the Monroe car, Ruditsky then telephoned the Villa Capri where he knew DiMaggio was dining. He told DiMaggio that he knew where Monroe was. DiMaggio and Sinatra discussed this animatedly, according to Bacon, who was watching them with interest. Suddenly DiMaggio rushed out of the Villa Capri, with Sinatra not far behind. Sanicola stayed with the rest of the Sinatra circle, eating and drinking.

It was DiMaggio who arrived at the scene first. Irwin greeted him. "He was very upset," Irwin said about DiMaggio. In fact, after a few moments of fast conversation, he walked rapidly away from Irwin, heading for the apartment. Irwin intercepted him. "I stopped him and tried to calm him down."

Almost immediately Sinatra arrived in his car. Inside the apartment, the landlady, Virginia Blasgen, looked out and saw the two men—"a tall one and a short one." The tall one, DiMaggio, was angry, she said. "The little one was jumping up and down and grinning at me."

Nothing happened for a while. But soon enough the action started. As yet Monroe, in the apartment of Sheila Stewart, was unaware of the drama outside. But soon enough she knew.

Sheila Stewart later said that everything suddenly began to happen. "It sounded like an army, a whole gang of people." She had been washing dishes at the time, while her guest sat in the dining room. "Marilyn didn't even get up," Stewart said.

But then there was the sound of splintering wood and crashing noises. By now Sinatra and DiMaggio were in the company of both detectives, plus a photographer who had been brought in to get pictures of the action. Flashes began popping; the bedroom burst into light. And there, in bed, watching her door come down, lay a terrified woman named Florence Kotz. She had been sound asleep before her door was splintered apart. She now began screaming.

There was a hurried consultation among the members of the raiding group outside her apartment, and then, abruptly, the hall was empty, with frantic men knocking into each other as they tried to flee the premises. "The DiMaggio war party," wrote

Summers, "searching for Marilyn, had blundered into the wrong apartment." It was forever to be known as the "Wrong Door Raid" in the history of Hollywood peccadilloes.

Sinatra had his own version of the raid, of course. He had to have one. In his version, he was sitting calmly in the car outside after failing to dissuade DiMaggio from crashing into the apartment in search of his wife—ex-wife—with whatever "lover" she might have.

And that was it.

Within minutes Hollywood knew about it. But most of the information was based on gossip, not facts. The police were in a quandary. To silence the gossips, they decided to write off the "raid" as a failed burglary attempt. It was three years later that Florence Kotz finally got up the nerve to sue, and the whole thing came out in public. Kotz sued for a large sum of money, and was awarded an out-of-court settlement of $7,500 to quiet her down.

But in all the court transcripts there was no mention of the actual "lover" Marilyn Monroe had been seeing at Sheila Stewart's apartment. Indeed Stewart was acting as a kind of "beard" to Monroe and her lover of the moment—a man named Hal Schaefer. Sheila Stewart later revealed that Schaefer was indeed with Marilyn that evening; Stewart had made dinner for both of them. When they heard the noise, the two lovers were alone in the dining room. "It was like somebody set off a bomb," Schaefer said. "The whole house shook. It was terrifying." Pause. "It was so lucky they got the wrong door. I think they would have done me terrible injury." To put it mildly.

What happened was that both Monroe and Schaefer

left the premises quickly in separate cars. Sinatra and DiMaggio went their separate ways, too, although DiMaggio managed to track down and confront his ex-wife before the night was out. Later, when the true facts began to surface, Sinatra and his lawyers hired Fred Otash, *another* hotshot Hollywood detective, to prove that Irwin was a liar, and that nobody could have recognized Sinatra on the lawn that night. Anyway, things fizzled out eventually, and the whole mess was forgotten. Schaefer was never named in any of the Hollywood publications. Shortly after the incident at Waring Street, Schaefer and Monroe talked on the phone.

"Perhaps one day, we'll meet again," she told him.

Schaefer knew they never would. "She told me she loved me, but I don't think she really knew what she meant," Schaefer said later.

Shortly after this fiasco, Marilyn Monroe was invited to stay at Sinatra's Coldwater Canyon residence, according to her conversations with Lena Pepitone, who acted as her maid-housekeeper in New York in 1957. Sinatra told Monroe that it would be easier for her to find a place of her own if she had a roof over her head while she was hunting. "Frankie and I had gotten to know each other a lot better," Monroe said, putting it in her usual understated manner. The two, of course, were later involved in a short-lived but memorable affair. "He had some funny ideas, too. He could be as jealous as Joe."

Marilyn Monroe had her own "funny" ideas, too. She loved to wander around the house—any house she was in at the time—without a stitch of clothing on. She would spend hours taking care of her hair.

Her public image was that of a "natural blonde," and of course it was an image right out of a bottle. She was naturally brown-haired.

Once her hair was bleached, she then began tinting her pubic hair to match. "You know, it has to match my hair," she once told Lena Pepitone. "With my white dresses and all, it just wouldn't look nice, to be dark down there. You could see through, you know."

"Is that safe, what you're doing?" Pepitone asked.

"It's a pain in the ass," Monroe said. "It burns and sometimes I get these infections. But what else can I do?"

Frank Sinatra did not mind in the least to have her meandering through the house naked—providing, of course, the two of them were alone. But whenever they had company, Monroe said, that was another matter altogether. Particularly, stag gatherings. On certain evenings Sinatra would have a group of friends over to play poker—sometimes members of the Clan, sometimes other associates. When it was stag night, Sinatra wanted Monroe to stay out of sight.

She was obviously bothered by the exclusion from the men's fun and games, but she did not protest. Instead, she kept to her room and listened to records, watched TV, and leafed through magazines. Or she drank. She once complained, "All there was to do was drink"—in spite of the magazines, the books, the records, and TV.

It was a difficult enough business in itself, trying to be social with members of Sinatra's Clan. Monroe was not au courant with the "in" jokes of the moment, and simply sat there with a blank look on her face as Sinatra and his friends—male and female—went on in their patented gibberish. "Stoned," as the Clan members might describe her.

One night during a hilarious card game at which Sinatra was officiating as "chairman of the board" and dealing the cards, Monroe drank a little too much and absentmindedly strolled out of her room in her usual costume—that is, stark naked—forgetful of her host's strict orders about wandering in the buff. She sauntered from one room to another until she finally opened the door to the room where the players were seated under a cloud of cigar and cigarette smoke.

Through the haze Sinatra saw her. Luckily, no one else noticed. He slammed down his drink and bounded across the room before anyone knew what he was up to. "He yanked me aside and ordered me to get my 'fat ass' back upstairs. How dare I embarrass him in front of his friends?"

Monroe tried to explain that she thought his friends might like a little companionship—maybe even a little bit of Monroe herself—more than their stupid cards. "He looked like he was going to kill me on the spot," she said. "I ran back to the bedroom and cried for hours. Here was Frankie being so nice to me, and I let him down."

But he was quick to forgive and forget. "No one in the whole world's sweeter than Frankie. When he came back later and kissed me on the cheek, that made me feel like a million. From then on, I *always* dressed up for him. Whether or not anyone was coming over."

The truth of the matter was that Marilyn liked men who could take charge of her, tell her what to do, dominate her.

"That's why Frankie and Joe are so great," she

once confided in her maid. "They're the boss. They run the show. I'm not very aggressive, but they sure are."

When she was told that Sinatra was skinny and weak looking, Monroe simply burst out laughing. "Oh, no," she said. "He's tough, real tough." The only problem with Sinatra was, she said, that she liked to go out on elegant evenings with him—but he never took her with him. "He always kept me in the bedroom."

Later on, after Monroe married Arthur Miller and then split up with him, Sinatra gave her a white French poodle as a gesture of sympathy over her marital troubles. Monroe named the poodle "Maf," short for "Mafia." Although Sinatra never thought it was a very funny joke, she loved to tease him about his "friends." "They all look like gangsters to me, even though they're not." Actually, she wanted to call the dog "The Mob," but Sinatra said it would make him look bad. "Nothing can make you look bad," Monroe told him. He agreed that the poodle could keep the name "Maf."

After spending some time at a psychiatric clinic in New York, Monroe flew back to California. Sinatra lent her his house. In June 1961 he was performing at the Sands Hotel in Las Vegas, and Monroe was there to watch him. She was in very good company—two of President Kennedy's sisters, Pat Lawford and Jean Smith. Eddie Fisher was there with his current wife, Elizabeth Taylor, watching the show. "Elizabeth and I sat in the audience with Dean and Jeanne Martin and Marilyn Monroe, who was having an affair with Sinatra, to watch his act," he wrote in his autobiography. "But all eyes were on Marilyn as she swayed back and forth to the music and pounded her hands on the stage, her breasts falling out of her low-cut dress. She was so beautiful—and so drunk. She came to the party later that evening, but Sinatra made no secret of his displeasure at her behavior and she vanished almost immediately."

Fisher was right about Sinatra and Monroe. They had become an "item" in the gossip columns. Sinatra discussed the rumors, telling Earl Wilson, "I just took Marilyn out a few times so she wouldn't be cooped up in her hotel."

About a month later she was on Sinatra's yacht, with a group of people including the Dean Martins and the Mike Romanoffs. Jeanne Martin said, "I remember going up to Frank's house before we got on the boat. And he said, 'Will you please go in and get Marilyn dressed so we can get in the limo and go?' She couldn't get herself organized."

Gloria Romanoff explained the problem. "She was taking sleeping pills, so she'd disappear at ten o'clock at night and not be awake till eleven or twelve the next day. We kidded Frank, saying, 'Some romance this is!'" Marilyn was wandering around on the dock, according to Jeanne Martin, trying to find more pills. "She'd be unable to sleep, and go lurching about half-dressed, trying to find someone who could give her 'reds' at three o'clock in the morning." When the yacht finally docked at the end of the trip, everyone stood about trying to figure out where to hold a get-together on shore. Monroe simply wandered off somewhere and vanished without saying good-bye to anybody.

There seemed no doubt that Monroe thought Sinatra was going to marry her. In September 1961 Monroe telephoned to her maid in New York and instructed her to fly out to the Coast to bring her a favorite $3,000 gown she had purchased earlier. She was invited to a big Hollywood affair and she was going to go out with Frank Sinatra. She wanted to look her best for him. "He likes me best when I'm all dressed up." None of the dresses she had bought in Beverly Hills was good enough. According to Lena Pepitone, "She was so close to a proposal, she felt, that she didn't want to take any risks."

The dress was an emerald-green-sequined evening gown that Monroe had had designed especially for her. "I've already told Frankie and he's all excited about seeing me in it." With her maid helping, Monroe dressed for the big benefit and looked at herself in the mirror. "Boy, wait till Frankie sees this!" she crowed. Her maid recalled that she must have stared at herself in the mirror for at least a half hour. And then, almost on cue, the doorbell rang, and Frank Sinatra stood there, looking snappy and suave as always, in full evening dress.

Monroe flew into the room, her platinum-tinted hair and green-sequined dress overpowering in the tiny apartment. Sinatra's face lit up. "Frankie!" she sighed, and went into his arms.

Lena Pepitone wrote: "They kissed like two people truly in love. They slowly drew apart to admire each other, Marilyn stroking the satin lapel of Frank's dinner jacket."

"Close your eyes," Sinatra told her.

Obediently, playfully, she did so. He took a small box out of his pocket and clipped two huge emerald earrings on her ears. Then he told her to open her eyes and look in the mirror.

"Oh, Frankie! Frankie!"

They kissed again, this time more passionately

than the first time. The maid was "embarrassed" to be watching them.

Frankie laughed, and casually said that the earrings cost $35,000. Monroe said later that she almost fainted at the price. But it was not an unusual gift for Sinatra to give to the woman he romanced.

The benefit was a tremendous success—and Sinatra and Monroe were the center of most of the attention. Every male there wanted to kiss Monroe; every woman wanted to kiss Sinatra. Tony Curtis and Billy Wilder were there—even Elizabeth Taylor.

Now Monroe was on fire to please Sinatra. She was going out with him every night. Every day she had the beauty people in to do her up. She was avid with anticipation and optimism. "Any day now," she would whisper to her maid. "Everything's working out just right. The dress was perfect! Frankie loved it!" And she would lounge around during the day, sleeping, drinking champagne, listening to Sinatra records, making telephone calls, visiting her doctor, playing with her dog Maf, and trying on clothes.

But it didn't work out with Sinatra. He was his own man, and he was elusive. Apparently he wasn't ready to settle down again. Although she had high hopes, Monroe instinctively realized that Sinatra was a hard man to land. When she was looking over some photographs of the yacht cruise she remarked to a friend, "I don't think I'll give [Frankie] copies. I think I've already given him enough."

A short time later she flew back to New York. Now she was on her pills again, brooding about Sinatra's rejection and worrying about getting a picture to make.

Meanwhile Sinatra was on the prowl for other

women in Hollywood. Juliet Prowse was just beginning to get a break as an actress, and her press agents dreamed up the idea of publicizing her legs. She was billed as the woman with the most beautiful legs in the entertainment business. Sinatra began going out with her so often that the gossip columns called their relationship a "steady" one.

When Monroe found out about this, she moaned, "How can Frankie do this?"

Things got worse. Soon references to an "engagement" between Prowse and Sinatra hit the gossip columns. At the same time, Sinatra continued calling Monroe and talking with her. "I can't tie him down, not Frankie," Marilyn Monroe moaned, "but I'll always love him."

Unknown to Monroe—or perhaps known but ignored—was the fact that Frank Sinatra lived by a code peculiarly his own. He was, essentially, a businessman. He acted at all times in conformity with his best business interests—even in his selection of women. In the last analysis, and if looked at in the proper light, his sexual attachments tended to be truly canny business ventures.

Cal York wrote about the Sinatra–Monroe relationship in *Photoplay*: "Everybody was so busy trying to make a serious romantic item out of the episodes that other scoops behind their meetings were overlooked. Frank, who always has a keen eye for business, arranged the dates to offer Marilyn a fantastic deal to co-star with him in a film for his own company." Sinatra obviously knew that by being seen around town with Monroe, public interest in them as a pair would be heightened. That in turn would serve as excellent advance publicity for a film collaboration.

Biographer Arnold Shaw speculated that the film Sinatra envisioned was a musical remake of *Born Yesterday*, in which Monroe would play the Judy Holliday role. Garson Kanin, the playwright, heard that Sinatra had offered a half million for the screen rights.

Of course, the movie never came off. Other and sadder events intervened.

Looked at in this light, even Sinatra's sudden switching to Juliet Prowse from Marilyn Monroe made sense. Perhaps he had sensed Monroe's growing desire to get married to him and made use of the Prowse episode to defuse her interest and signal to her that it was not a serious affair.

Eventually Marilyn Monroe was assigned to a motion picture titled *Something's Got to Give*, a remake of an old Cary Grant hit, *My Favorite Wife*. She moved to Hollywood again, but things were clearly going to pieces for her.

Although she flew to Tahoe to stay at the Cal-Neva Lodge, owned by Frank Sinatra, and flew there in Sinatra's plane, she was not really going out with him anymore. She was in fact involved with President Jack Kennedy and with his brother, Attorney General Bobby Kennedy. A lot of the shenanigans at Cal-Neva hit the gossip columns.

Joe DiMaggio, working at a lucrative new job in New York, was still in love with Marilyn Monroe. Nunnally Johnson, the scriptwriter on *Something's Got to Give*, tried to get DiMaggio to come to the Coast to help Marilyn find herself.

But DiMaggio was so enraged about the happenings at Lake Tahoe that he wouldn't do it. He thought that a lot of the blame for the drugs and the gadding about, since much of it took place in Sinatra's plane, was due to Sinatra's influence.

It wasn't.

Something else—something quite different—was happening with Monroe.

Abruptly DiMaggio quit his job in New York, got in touch with Monroe, and flew out to Tahoe. It seemed as if they had patched things up and were on the road to a reconciliation, perhaps even a remarriage. But it did not happen. Within days, Marilyn Monroe was dead of an overdose of drugs. Her last words to Peter Lawford, who talked to her on the telephone the night she died, were significant ones:

"Say good-bye to Pat, say good-bye to the president." Note: not to the attorney general—but to the president.

After her death, suddenly her Hollywood and Washington "friends" were not around anymore. It fell, almost by default, to DiMaggio to take care of her interment. He said little, but when he did talk, he fulminated about the Kennedys, the Clan, and especially, about Sinatra.

Sinatra was in shock for weeks after her death, according to George Jacobs, his valet. "He called me and said, 'Let's get out of here,' and we went down to Palm Springs."

The Kennedys had moved into Sinatra's life—and they turned out to be people he couldn't quite cope with or control. And, because he couldn't, a number of tragic things happened—to him, and to people he had come to care about.

★ 9 ★

The Kennedy
Disconnection

From his early days in New Jersey Frank Sinatra
had always espoused liberal causes. And he had
always honored his mother's position in the Democratic party by voting that ticket and supporting
her political cohorts. He had been a supporter of
Franklin D. Roosevelt, naming his son Franklin
after the president—although because his son was
called Frank, Jr., many people mistakenly assumed
his name was Francis. Like most Italians in New
Jersey during that period, he was a Democrat to
the core and never considered voting any other way.

He had supported Adlai Stevenson in his losing
bids in the presidency in 1952 and 1956. Yet now,
with Eisenhower unable to succeed himself and with
Vice-President Nixon lacking the kind of biparti-
san support that had helped elect Eisenhower, it
looked as if John F. Kennedy might just win the
election if he had enough help. Sinatra was a natural to support Kennedy, if Kennedy could get himself nominated. Not only was Frank a good friend of
Peter Lawford, who was married to one of Kennedy's sisters, but he had met and liked the Kennedy
brothers. Yet before this could happen, Sinatra found

himself in the strange position of doing a "liberal" thing and at the same time endangering the "liberal" cause.

In the general excitement over the dangers of communism in the 1950s, a group of Hollywood screen writers—later called the Hollywood Ten—were jailed for contempt of Congress during an investigation into alleged subversive influences in the movie business. One of them, Albert Maltz, had served his time but had been unable to get work in Hollywood afterward because of his stand against Congress. Sinatra had worked with Maltz on *The House I Live In*, which Maltz had written. In 1960 Sinatra purchased the screen rights to William Bradford Huie's *The Execution of Private Slovik*, the story of the first American G.I. to be executed since Civil War times—he was accused of desertion in World War II—and he hired Maltz to write the screenplay.

In March 1960 the story of Maltz's hiring came out in the newspapers—and all hell broke loose. The Hearst newspapers claimed that Sinatra's actions might well sound the death knell for Kennedy's chances for the Democratic nomination. When John Wayne was asked for his opinion of Sinatra and Maltz, he said, "I don't think my opinion is too important. Why don't you ask Sinatra's crony, who's going to run our country for the next few years, what *he* thinks of it?" Sinatra responded in a paid ad in the *New York Times*, titled "A Statement of Fact." He said that connecting candidate Kennedy to Sinatra's decision to hire Matlz was "hitting below the belt." He went on: "I make movies. I do not ask the advice of Senator Kennedy on whom I should hire. . . . I have, in my opinion, hired the best man for the job."

Independently, the *New York Times* editorialized: "This marks the first time that a top movie star has defied the rule laid down [thirteen years before] by the major movie studios." In general, the liberal press applauded him—which did little good to attract middle-of-the-roaders to the Democratic cause. But of course most of the noise came from the opposition. One of the Hearst papers accused Sinatra of allowing a "real Communist pro" to insinuate the "Communist line" into a script. Hedda Hopper wrote: "If Sinatra loves his country he won't do this." Harry Cohn was his usual foulmouthed self, yelling at Sinatra: "They're calling you a fucking Communist!"

Behind the scenes a number of things were happening. Peter Lawford was developing a television series called *The Bachelor* in which he intended to have Sinatra and members of the Clan appear; about this time, the sponsor, Pontiac Motors, pulled out of the deal. Also, the banks were giving Frank Sinatra a bad time over lending the money to finance the film, despite Sinatra's impressive track record in movies over the past decade.

One other thing either happened or didn't. Either Joseph P. Kennedy did or did not get in touch with Frank Sinatra directly to offer him the alternative of getting rid of Maltz or of jumping off the John F. Kennedy bandwagon. And what actually happened as the result of all this backstage maneuvering?

Early in April a statement was issued from Sinatra's place in Palm Springs. This is the way it is was worded:

"Due to the reactions of my family, my friends and the American public, I have instructed my attorneys to make a settlement with Albert Maltz and to inform him he will not write the screenplay for *The Execution of Private Slovik*. I had thought the major consideration was whether or not the resulting script would be in the best interests of the United States. Since my conversation with Mr. Maltz had indicated that he had an affirmative, pro-American approach to the story and since I felt fully capable as producer of enforcing such standards, I have defended my hiring of Mr. Maltz. But the American public has indicated that it feels the morality of hiring Mr. Maltz is the more crucial matter, and I will accept the majority opinion."

It was not Frank Sinatra's finest hour.

Albert Maltz spoke about the incident. "He [Sinatra] was prepared to fight. His eyes were open. The ad firing me was ridiculous. The American people had not spoken; only the Hearst press and the American Legion had. Something had come from behind that caused him to change his position."

In one of Maltz's scrapbooks was pasted a clipping from a Dorothy Kilgallen column. "The real credit [for what happened to Maltz] belongs to former Ambassador Joseph P. Kennedy," Kilgallen wrote. "Unquestionably anti-Communist, Dad Kennedy would have invited Frank to jump off the Jack Kennedy Presidental bandwagon if he hadn't unloaded Mr. Maltz."

Sinatra tried to make up for this incident at the Democratic Convention in July by involving as many friends as he could to help John Fitzgerald Kennedy. Once Kennedy became the presidential candidate, Sinatra and his people went at it full-tilt. Sinatra's contribution was a recording of the song

"High Hopes," which became the official Kennedy campaign song.

One of their rallies took place at the Sands Hotel in Las Vegas, where Kennedy was photographed with Sinatra. Later, the candidate appeared with Sinatra. Dean Martin did his inebriated Dino bit, and joked: "What was the last name?" Another of the Clan carried in Sammy Davis, Jr., announcing that he had just been delivered from the N.A.A.C.P. The Sunday *New York Daily News* ran a piece about Sinatra's friends, which opened with this sentence: "One question which will be answered once and for all by the 1960 Presidential campaign is: Can a man whose brother-in-law is a member of the Clan be elected President of the United States?" Joe Hyams immediately wrote that Sinatra's Clan had become a "political casualty."

There was immediate and powerful reaction to this. Kennedy insiders from the Cape swooped down on Vegas and quickly tried to confiscate and destroy all the photographs and negatives showing Kennedy at play with Sinatra and members of the Clan.

In August Sinatra responded to the brouhaha, sounding strangely subdued. He told the press that labeling his friend members of "the Clan" was ridiculous. There was no such thing as "the Clan." "It's a figment of someone's imagination," he said. "Naturally, people in Hollywood socialize with friends, as they do in any community. But we do not get together in childish fraternities, as some people would like to think." Later, Dorothy Kilgallen wrote that the presidential candidate had begun protesting newspaper items that linked him with Sinatra. "He's no friend of mine, he's just a friend of

Pat . . . and Peter Lawford," she quoted the candidate as saying. But: "So last week the Democratic candidate for the presidency was guest of honor at a private little dinner given by Frank," Kilgallen went on. "No reason why he shouldn't, of course—but why try to kid the press?"

One of the key members of the Clan was, of course, Sinatra's longtime friend Sammy Davis, Jr. As it happened, Davis had recently fallen in love with May Britt, a beautiful Swedish actress who was beginning to make her mark in Hollywood, and was planning to marry her. Sinatra agreed to act as best man. The media observers were amused. One called the upcoming nuptials "secret Republican strategy." Davis, realizing what this interracial marriage might mean to the Kennedy campaign, immediately postponed the wedding, apologizing to Sinatra and those who had already received wedding invitations. Sinatra understood what was going on; he insisted that the wedding proceed no matter what. But Davis and his bride-to-be finally sent out an announcement postponing the wedding "due to a legal technicality in Miss Britt's Mexican divorce from her previous husband."

Once the election was won, the Kennedys announced that the inaugural gala would be produced by Peter Lawford and Frank Sinatra. And the opposition press joined in immediately, speculating on Clan appointees to the Kennedy cabinet: Sinatra as ambassador to Italy or secretary of trouble; Sammy Davis, Jr., as ambassador to Israel, or, by default, ambassador to Kenya; Dean Martin as secretary of liquor. "The Rat Pack may be making a nest for itself in the White House after next January 20," wrote a worried Ruth Montgomery.

The inaugural gala began with Sinatra under the guns of the press, all now aimed at him. When he and Lawford rode in from the airport, the press pointed out that they had been transported in a limousine chauffeured by a G.I. Later, Sinatra canceled a meeting with a women's group that wanted to throw a champagne party for the performers—and heard about it loud and clear from women reporters. Some of the writers muttered darkly about the fact that Sinatra did not provide "the proper cultural tone" to the affair.

On January 19, the day of the gala, it began to snow, crippling transportation in the capital for hours. "Those Republicans are sure poor losers," Joey Bishop said. In the concert hall, half of the hundred-man orchestra and its conductor and soloist were missing. But the show itself was a huge success. Close to $1.5 million was raised to wipe out the national committee's campaign deficit. When it was over, the president-elect said: "We're all indebted to a great friend, Frank Sinatra. Long before he could sing, he was pulling votes in a New Jersey precinct. . . . Tonight, we saw excellence." Sinatra responded: "I only wish my kids could have seen it. I can't find the words. . . ."

After the inauguration ceremonies, Sinatra held his own private party. In the middle of it Peter Lawford appeared, and told Frank: "The president would like to have you join his party." It was obvious that it was a royal summons.

"Tell him we're eating," Sinatra responded casually.

Edward G. Robinson, who was present, murmured, "You're going to see a wop get nailed to the door."

Oh?

Some minutes later there was a hush over the crowd and Sinatra looked up to see the president of the United States in the room with him. "I'm sorry," President Kennedy said. "I didn't know you were eating."

Everything got ironed out finally. Later Sinatra thought about Kennedy's unexpected appearance, and smiled.

"*That's* class!" he said.

The following morning, Sinatra and the Lawfords breakfasted with Robert F. Kennedy, then flew to Palm Beach with Joseph P. Kennedy, where they all relaxed in the sunshine. It seemed almost inevitable that Sinatra and JFK should get along very well together. They had a common religion, they had a common interest in women, they had a taste for glamour and loved to have *fun*.

Sinatra's womanizing was well known. Not so well known was Kennedy's. Both Kennedys. All three Kennedys, for that matter.

President Kennedy had once confided in Clare Boothe Luce, playwright and wife of the publisher of *Time*: "Dad told all the boys to get laid as often as possible." Following this advice as best he could, Jack became known in his navy days as "Shafty." When he got to the White House, he felt there was no reason for him to change his tricks. "Sex to Jack Kennedy," said Nancy Dickerson, a Washington reporter, "was like another cup of coffee."

And of course all the Kennedys were fascinated with the world that Frank Sinatra inhabited—the world of Hollywood. Their own father had indulged himself in Hollywood years before, even carrying on a highly publicized affair with Gloria Swanson. In the 1940s and 1950s, John Kennedy dated numerous stars and starlets like Gene Tierney, Sonja Henie, Angela Greene, Kim Novak, Janet Leigh, and Rhonda Fleming. Robert Kennedy befriended Judy Garland—among others.

Now that John Kennedy was president, they had a base of operations on the West Coast—the beach property of the Kennedy brother-in-law, Peter Lawford. Although Lawford was the link between the Kennedys of Washington and Marilyn Monroe, it was thought that Jack had probably met Monroe through Frank Sinatra.

In fact, the original Kennedy–Monroe connection was made in the 1950s, when Jack was Senator Kennedy. "He was unknown here, relatively speaking," said Arthur James, a real-estate agent who knew Marilyn Monroe in the late forties and fifties. "He and Marilyn could get away with a great deal. They sometimes drank at the Malibu Cottage, which was the raunchiest place you've seen in your life. It was just a bar, with maybe eight stools, and sawdust on the floor, but in those days it was a hangout for some of the most famous names in Hollywood." James said he once saw John Kennedy walking on the shore with Marilyn near the Malibu pier; Monroe told him that she and Kennedy used rooms at the Holiday House Motel in Malibu, and at another hotel where Sunset Boulevard intersects with what was then the Pacific Coast Highway.

Phyllis McGuire, one of the singing McGuire sisters, and a friend of Sinatra, knew the Kennedys well from earlier days.

"The initial relationship [between the Kennedy brothers and Marilyn Monroe] was with John," she said. "And there definitely was a relationship with Bob. . . . They were seen together at their little hideaways. And, you know, that's very like the Kennedys, just to pass it down from one to the other—Joe Kennedy to John, Jack to Bobby, Bobby to Ted. That's just the way they did things."

And so the chain for women apparently went something like this: Frank Sinatra > Peter Lawford > John Kennedy > Robert Kennedy > Teddy Kennedy.

But there was a problem in this particular case. Monroe's associations were many, but mostly routine, with one particular exception. She had, in the course of her peregrinations in the Hollywood jungles, met Johnny Roselli, a mobster who had worked for Longy Zwillman's gang in New Jersey. After moving to Chicago, he became an adept at extortion and labor racketeering for Al Capone. Roselli then moved on to Hollywood, where he joined the International Alliance of Theatrical Stage Employees and Moving Picture Machine Operators, a union of Hollywood blue-collar technicians. Convicted of extortion for racketeering activities in the union, he had then served time for four years.

Roselli was an intimate of Sam Giancana, *the* Chicago Mafia *capo*—in other words, its big honcho. He had a great deal of clout in Hollywood, not only with the studio managers, but with the entertainers as well. His power reached into MGM, Twentieth Century–Fox, Paramount, and Warner Brothers. And, of course, it reached into the casinos of Las Vegas; they were playgrounds for the Hollywood set. Roselli, in fact, had lent money to Harry Cohn, for whom Monroe and Sinatra had made several pictures at Columbia. Interestingly enough, Roselli and Cohn wore identical ruby rings—Cohn's actually provided to him by Roselli.

According to Joseph Shimon, a former police inspector in Washington, D.C., "Roselli met Monroe. He met her socially, he knew a lot of her friends, and he knew her close business associates." Many of these facts were known to the FBI and members of the justice department. And Robert Kennedy had become head of the justice department. These files were open to him.

Earl Wilson pointed out that even in 1960, during the campaign, the Kennedys realized that Frank Sinatra could be a liability to them. A Constitutional Rights Conference had been sponsored by the Kennedys in New York, with Sinatra invited to join. But Harris Wofford, the Kennedys' civil-rights adviser, recommended that Sinatra be excluded. John L. Seigenthaler, another adviser, suggested that the then-candidate not be seen with Sinatra "in public."

Once installed in the office of attorney general, Robert Kennedy began looking deeply into the files and tracking the paths of people linked to members of the mob. For example: Marilyn Monroe's connection with Johnny Roselli. Another link was made by Phyllis McGuire, who knew Sinatra well, and later became mobster Sam Giancana's lover. Sinatra had helped McGuire get a small role in his movie *Come Blow Your Horn*. But why had he hired her for the job? Because of his own assessment of her talents? Or had Giancana leaned on him to get her the job? Later on, reports of the Federal Bureau of Investigation showed that indeed Giancana *had* used pressure on Sinatra to secure McGuire the job.

As far as Robert Kennedy was concerned, racketeers and mobsters were very definitely the "bad guys." It was almost an obsession with him, which could to some extent be traced back to his father's experiences. The Kennedys had always been a closely knit family. Father, mother, sons, and daughters— all were linked together. And the leader of the family was the father. What Papa said was law.

In the patriarch's earlier years—in 1927, to be exact—Joe Kennedy had run a very profitable operation smuggling in bonded Scotch whisky from Britain to Boston and then peddling it up and down the East Coast. Naturally, this activity was illegal because of the Prohibition. But Kennedy felt the law was more or less unjustified. Kennedy worked the operation from the States, but he had agents in Scotland, and shippers who took the stuff clandestinely from Scotland, through Ireland, and landed it secretly near Boston.

Kennedy was not the only one running a bit of illegal Scotch into the States in direct conflict with the law. Members of the mob were too. Lucky Luciano and Frank Costello joined forces to set up a very efficient bootleg network that brought the stuff right into New York City.

A convoy of Kennedy's whisky en route from Ireland to Boston was hijacked by a gang of Luciano's organization waiting along the roadside in southern New England. The Kennedy guards resisted, and a bloody battle wiped out nearly every one of the Kennedy group. Luciano wound up with the liquor. Kennedy lost a fortune in the hijack, and was obliged to provide financial help to the widows and relatives of the guards killed in the action. One of Luciano's men said: "It really wasn't our fault. Those Irish idiots hire amateurs as guards."

The theory was, according to mobster Doc Stacher, that "If there was a chance of getting out of an ambush, then of course you had to fight. But if you were outnumbered or outgunned, and in a position where you couldn't do anything about it, our soldiers were always told to run or surrender." Kennedy's "soldiers" didn't. And Kennedy somehow found out who had done him in. Certainly he became bitter about this messy operation. Although he took no immediate action—there was little he could do—he brooded about it for years. Certainly he told his children, and undoubtedly the men in the family empathized with his feelings.

Robert Kennedy apparently felt it more deeply than the rest of the brood. Crime fighting was in his blood. He had whetted his appetite for that kind of power in the years when he had served as counsel for his brother, Senator John F. Kennedy, who had chaired the Senate Labor Rackets Select Committee. It was here that he was able to zero in on the enemy, as he saw the enemy: the racketeers of America. In fact, out of his experience had come a book about crime and unionism—*The Enemy Within*—which had appeared in 1960. It certainly did not hurt his brother John F. Kennedy's chances at the high office he aspired to.

Now, in the seat of judicial power in Washington, this racket buster par excellence was in a position to *do* something about it, and from the very top. Now he would be able to pay back all those racketeers who had taken advantage of his father in those long-gone days of Prohibition. Now who would have the last laugh?

Frank Sinatra saw Robert Kennedy as a swinging womanizer every bit as active as his older brother Jack and his younger brother Teddy, and considered him a good friend. So what if his own women occasionally connected up with hoodlums? Who didn't? And what was wrong with seeing a man with a record occasionally—as long as you yourself kept clean?

But he had misread Robert Kennedy—misread him badly. Maybe Bobby bent the marriage law a bit, but he would never bend a criminal law. And to be linked with a known criminal was anathema to him. In fact, from the beginning, Bobby was worried about his brother Jack's associations with various people.

There was Monroe—who *was* friendly with Johnny Roselli. And there was Phyllis McGuire, whom Jack didn't know, but whom Sinatra did. And Bobby knew *she* was sleeping with Sam Giancana. And then it all came to a head in an ironic way because of a woman named Judith Katherine Immoor, who worked at Paramount Studios.

Frank Sinatra had become interested in Immoor, who went under her married name of Campbell, even though she was divorced. In November 1959 Sinatra had invited her to Honolulu where he was taking a short holiday with Peter Lawford, Pat Kennedy Lawford, and several other close friends. There at Waikiki Sinatra and Campbell enjoyed an affair, which continued for some months afterward.

In February 1960 Senator John F. Kennedy and his brother Teddy were at the Sands to see Frank Sinatra perform. The Lawfords were there, too, all sitting at Sinatra's special table. So was Judith Campbell. Sinatra introduced the senator to her.

The senator was smitten with Judy and began an affair that continued until the spring of 1962—from the time he was a senator through the time he was a candidate for the presidency and during part of the time he was president.

No problem would have existed if Sinatra had not, some months after beginning his affair with her, introduced Judy Campbell to Sam Giancana, the Windy City *capo,* down in Florida, where he was performing and where Judy was visiting him. Campbell did not even know Giancana's real name. To her he was simply Sam Flood. But while she continued her affairs with Sinatra and the senator (later the president), she also began one with Giancana. Simultaneously.

That is getting ahead of the story, though.

In 1961 comedian Jerry Lewis, ex-partner of Dean Martin, became involved in a messy divorce action brought by a man married to a starlet named Judy Meredith (not to be confused with Judy Campbell). Lewis had been named as one of the men in Judy Meredith's life. The comedian was working at Paramount Studios at the time, and Judith Campbell was a member of his office staff. Lewis knew that during this period Campbell was running around with Sam Giancana, the Chicago mobster. Lewis called in Campbell. He wanted her to request that Sam Giancana intervene with private eye Fred Otash, who was handling the Meredith divorce investigation, to expunge Lewis's name from the evidence that was being presented for the trial. This was done.

Otash later said that there were "other names" in the records he had, including those of Dean Martin, Frank Sinatra, and—John F. Kennedy! Otash met in 1961 with Johnny Roselli, a meeting held "at the request of the Attorney General." Otash claimed that Roselli asked him to remove the president's name from the divorce evidence, in addition to the name of Jerry Lewis.

The attorney general was at that time involved in Hollywood with the movie production of his exposé of Hoffa and the mob, *The Enemy Within*. Jerry Wald, who had produced two Monroe films earlier, was assigned to the picture at Twentieth Century– Fox. Suddenly Wald got an anonymous telephone call. "Are you the son of a bitch who is going to photograph *The Enemy Within*?" This didn't deter Wald. Paul Newman was cast as the star, and the attorney general kept coming to script conferences.

In November 1961, the FBI received a letter of proof that the president was an adulterer, "including photographs." A few days before that, President Kennedy had allowed himself to be seen in public with Monroe at his side at the Beverly Hilton Hotel.

But, more than that, in February 1962 FBI surveillance on Roselli, apparently instituted at the behest of Robert Kennedy, determined that Judith Campbell was simultaneously carrying on affairs with both the president of the United States *and* mobster Sam Giancana. Within weeks of that surveillance, specifically on March 22, 1962, J. Edgar Hoover lunched with President Kennedy. A search of the White House phone log later determined that from that date, the president, who had been in contact with Judith Campbell frequently, never called her again. However, Campbell later said that she continued to see President Kennedy for months after that time, in spite of Hoover's warnings about the compromising position in which the president was placing himself.

In fact, J. Edgar Hoover's warnings had only stimulated Kennedy to mutter disdainfully to Kenneth

O'Donnell: "Get rid of that bastard. He's the biggest bore."

Of course, it didn't happen, but things were coming to a head. The attorney general, still obsessed with the proximity of mobsters to the Oval Office, as noted in his FBI reports, and still determined to bring down as many racketeers and hoods as he could through the machinery of the justice department, noted that one name kept recurring and recurring in these reports. That name was Frank Sinatra. Frank Sinatra > Marilyn Monroe > John F. Kennedy > Johnny Roselli. Frank Sinatra > Phyllis McGuire > Sam Giancana. Frank Sinatra > Judith Campbell > John F. Kennedy > Sam Giancana. There were wheels within wheels. There were women and men and more women—and some of these chains led right up to the Oval Office.

In *Mafia Princess* Antoinette Giancana made the following remark about this "connection": "How was I to know that . . . Sam [Giancana], introduced to a woman by Frank Sinatra, would have a coast-to-coast affair with that woman, Judith [Campbell] Exner, while she was secretly having an affair with President John F. Kennedy."

It was about this time in the spring of 1962 that Joseph P. Kennedy invited Sinatra and members of the Clan to visit him on the French Riviera where he was vacationing. A few days later, the invitation was inexplicably withdrawn. It was believed by the press that the White House itself had called off the ambassador. Well. The White House—or the justice department.

Peter Lawford hosted a fete at his beachfront house in Malibu about this time at which the president, the attorney general, Marilyn Monroe, and

Frank Sinatra were present—along with others. They were sitting around the palatial home—it had once belonged to Louis B. Mayer—when there was an unexpected interruption.

Actually, the president was enjoying himself tremendously, being away from the pressure of his high office. Jackie and the children were not with him. It was fun time, with jokes, and anecdotes, and drinking, and horsing around. But according to Sidney Skolsky, one member of the party was very quiet: the attorney general. Usually the master of incisive comments, he was at this point brooding deeply about something that seemed to be gnawing at him internally. There were smiles all around, a short silence after a particularly funny exchange, and then the attorney general cleared his throat. "Jack," he said to his brother, as if the words were being forced to come out from somewhere deep within him—some deep and dark corner where he had examined them one by one and finally determined their worth.

There was the proper quiet.

"You can't be friends with Sinatra," Robert Kennedy finally said, glancing from the singer to the President.

The room grew very still. All present seemed frozen in their chairs. Sinatra was gazing at the attorney general as if he did not recognize him.

"You can't have him coming in the front door or the side door of the White House."

Only the sound of ice in the drinks broke the silence.

"You can't stay at his house, you can't pal around with him," Robert Kennedy continued. "Not while I'm investigating activities in Vegas."

Sinatra stared stonily at the attorney general, his face visibly drawn.

"The thing, Jack, is that you can't walk on both sides of the road." Robert Kennedy shook the ice in his cocktail glass. "If Sinatra's your friend and visits you in the White House and you see him in Palm Springs, then I have to stop all my investigations and resign as attorney general."

The president continued to drink, but said nothing. The burden of silence was crushing. The party was over. Within a short time, everybody began to say good-bye.

Yet on the surface, nothing changed. The romance between the Sinatra group and the Kennedys seemed to be continuing. It was announced in the press that Frank Sinatra was going to have the president of the United States as his house guest during JFK's next trip to the West Coast. It was a tremendous honor. Sinatra immediately gave orders to build a new wing on the house for the president and guest houses for the presidential entourage, including the Secret Service.

The house, which had originally had two bedrooms, had now grown into a compound with a dining room capable of feeding forty or fifty people. Not only Sinatra but the entire Palm Springs area was beside itself with excitement. Obviously, the little exchange between the attorney general and the president at Lawford's place in Malibu had been nothing but simple jawboning.

The construction concluded, the interior decorating concluded, all was in readiness . . .

Consternation!

At the last moment, the president's plans shifted. Instead of stopping off at Frank Sinatra Drive in

Palm Springs, the president and his entourage were going to stay at the Shadow Mountain residence of Bing Crosby in Palm Desert. "And that fucking Bing isn't even a Democrat!" one of Sinatra's friends cried in shocked surprise.

A statement released to the press on March 25, 1962, announced that the Secret Service had made the final decision to change the itinerary. The Crosby bungalow, fifteen miles from downtown Palm Springs was, in their opinion, more defensible than Sinatra's sprawling compound.

Defensible from what?

What burned Sinatra up was the fact that Lawford's smiling face was in all the publicity shots taken at Crosby's place during the president's visit. "Peter should have delivered Jack," a Sinatra intimate said sternly. Lawford claimed that he was unable to influence the Secret Service. "The Secret Service was afraid the security available at Frank's place was just not adequate. Bing's place was better from that standpoint. And Jimmy Van Heusen's house nearby was excellent for the security headquarters."

To cool things down, the president made a personal telephone call to Sinatra from Crosby's place. He wanted him to come to Bing's to see him. Sinatra said that it was impossible. "I'm on my way to L.A. Sorry I can't make it now." He had been snubbed. He knew what to do about a snub. He took it from the president's own famous file of sayings.

"Don't get mad, get even."

He did so—later.

But now he was hurting. Had it been because Jackie Kennedy didn't want to be associated with him? Was it because Bobby was afraid the presidential tie-in with Judith Campbell *and* Sam Giancana might become public knowledge? Was it because of hints of the Kennedy–Monroe affair?

Actually, in the long run, Sinatra wasn't as shaken by the event as he could have been. He held nothing against the president; the man he loathed was the attorney general.

In the Palm Springs house a plaque was mounted— in spite of what had happened:

JOHN F. KENNEDY SLEPT HERE NOVEMBER 6TH AND
7TH, 1960

In memory, of course, of happier times—before Kennedy became president.

When John F. Kennedy was assassinated in November 1963, Sinatra did not appear at the funeral.

He telephoned the White House from California, offering his condolences.

Patricia Lawford took his call.

★ 10 ★

The Empire Builder

A longtime intimate of frustration and rejection, Frank Sinatra did not let the Kennedy snub deter him from his own work. Although he could no longer channel his energies into fund raising and political activities for and with the Kennedys, he turned to his own interests and began consolidating the huge business empire he had begun to construct in the early 1960s.

Briefly, these enterprises included his own record label, the production and direction of motion pictures, part ownership in numerous casinos; at one point even the possibility of starting a talent agency was under consideration.

Although estimates of the Sinatra fortune were wild at best, they hovered somewhere around $50 million in 1976, with one pundit speculating that even in the 1960s he was grossing $20 million a year.

In 1965, *Newsweek* magazine listed the known businesses of Sinatra's wide-ranging empire. They included:

- Artanis Productions, an organization in which Warner Brothers had minority holdings, with

Sinatra the majority. Artanis produced *None But the Brave,* which Sinatra directed, and *Marriage on the Rocks,* among others. Artanis, is, of course, "Sinatra" spelled backward.

- Park Lake Enterprises, another production company outside the Warner Brothers organization. Sinatra produced *4 for Texas, Robin and the Seven Hoods,* and *Von Ryan's Express* for it.
- Reprise Records, a record-producing company of which Sinatra owned one-third; Warner Brothers owned the other two-thirds.
- Cal Jet Airway, a charter airline that operated one Lear, one five-place Alouette helicopter, and one three-place Morane-Saulnier; a $600,000 Lear was on order.
- Titanium Metal Forming Company, a firm that manufactured metal parts for aircraft and missile builders.

Sinatra also owned extensive real-estate holdings in Arizona and California, as well as the Cal-Neva Lodge at Lake Tahoe, a resort establishment then appraised at $4 million dollars which he did not operate at the time of the *Newsweek* article. And although it was not generally known by the public, Sinatra also held a 9 percent interest in the Sands Hotel in Las Vegas.

With the growing concern of Attorney General Robert Kennedy about mob operations in the United States, surveillance on known gangsters and members of the Mafia was increased dramatically. Since the death of many of the principals, tapes of these extensive surveillances have been made available to the public, and a great deal of the inside details about Mafia operations that were only hinted at then are now known.

For example, it was known by most insiders at that time—the early sixties—that the Sands Hotel was controlled by the mob. Mob ownership was nothing new for the hostelry. It had been owned by more different gangs than any other casino in Nevada—gangs from such diverse cities as Houston, Galveston, New York City, Newark, St. Louis, Los Angeles, Minneapolis, San Francisco, Chicago, Cleveland, Detroit, Jersey City, Miami, and New Orleans.

Joseph (Doc) Stacher, a former New Jersey gangster—he had been at one time or another a hijacker, a bootlegger, and a drug dealer—was the man who built the Sands. Interviewed after being deported to Israel, Stacher talked extensively about his life in crime. Of the Sands, he said: "To make sure we'd get enough top-level investors, we brought George Raft into the deal and sold Frank Sinatra a 9 percent stake in the hotel. Frank was flattered to be invited, but the object was to get him to perform there, because there's no bigger draw in Las Vegas. When Frankie was performing, the hotel really filled up."

Why Sinatra, who knew the danger of dealing with mobsters, agreed to put money into the operation always puzzled many of his fans. A *Newsweek* writer discussed Sinatra's penchant for associating with mobsters in the following manner: "There is some pseudo-psychiatric speculation that Sinatra needs the occasional company of dubious characters because he was never as tough a youth as his press agentry once implied. It may be that he simply enjoys it."

Antoinette Giancana, the daughter of mobster *capo* Sam Giancana, wrote in her book *Mafia Princess* that her father knew that Sinatra liked tough guys and liked to pal around with them. "I've heard Sam say on many occasions that Frank was a frustrated gangster," she added.

Anyway, Sinatra owned more stock in the Sands than anyone else but Jack Entratter. A friend of Sinatra's for years, Entratter had started out as a bouncer at the Copacabana when Sinatra was singing there; he worked the Stork Club too, where he was known as Mr. Six-by-Six-Plus.

According to Ed Reid and Ovid Demaris in *The Green Felt Jungle*, Entratter was allegedy the "front" man for Frank Costello and Joey Adonis, two powerful Mafia figures. Costello, born Francesco Castiglia in Sicily in 1891, was known as the "prime minister" of organized crime in America.

Entratter began at the Sands as show producer and general manager of the Copa Room. In the late 1950s he became president of the organization. At that time his percentage in the casino soared from 5 percent to 12 percent; he became a millionaire.

But the real "inside" top man at the Sands was not Entratter but Doc Stacher, its originator. It certainly did not seem to bother Sinatra that Stacher, a known gangster, was a fellow stockholder in the hotel.

According to the *New York Times* expert on organized crime, Nicholas Gage, Robert Kennedy had a nineteen-page report prepared concerning Sinatra's activities with mobsters. In that report, government investigators determined that Sinatra was in contact with perhaps ten of the best-known gangsters in the country in the fifties and sixties. The Fischetti brothers have already been mentioned, and they figure in the report. In Skokie, Illinois, a car dealer wanted Sinatra to make a singing commercial for his agency. Sinatra ignored the request. But then the Fischetti brothers stepped into the picture. Sinatra changed his mind and made the commercial. Later he said that he did it as a favor to the car dealer. In fact, Sinatra accepted two Pontiacs as a gift from the dealer. Oddly enough, Joseph Fischetti was seen shortly after this, driving through town with a close girlfriend of his brother Rocco in a car bearing the dealer's license plate and label.

In April 1962 Joe Fischetti—using his usual alias of Joe Fisher—received seventy-one checks from the Fontainebleau Hotel, each in the amount of $540 (total, $38,340). In his income tax, Fischetti listed the money as earnings for acting as the hotel's "talent agent."

Later, Sinatra reportedly lent Fischetti $90,000 to help him buy an interest in a large Miami restaurant. Sinatra was reported to entertain at the Fontainebleau in Miami Beach at a contract price plus a cash deal, handled by Fischetti.

The report also stated: "In Miami Beach, Fischetti is Sinatra."

Cal-Neva was apparently Sinatra's favorite place. Of course, he owned it—but there was more. It was a beautiful spot right on Lake Tahoe, isolated from city crowds and traffic. Situated directly on the California–Nevada border—which went through the middle of the hotel—it took its strange name from that fact. On the California side were the capacious dining room and the coffee shop. On the Nevada side were the casinos, where visitors could gamble to their hearts' content. Lake Tahoe and the surrounding ski resorts made an ideal setting for the beautiful lodge. The same entertainers who appeared in Las Vegas appeared at Cal-Neva to lure in the crowds.

Sinatra's ownership of Cal-Neva was not total, according to FBI records. In fact, he owned 36.6 percent in the hostelry—more than anyone else, but still not all. He shared it with various other owners, one of them being Sam Giancana. (It was Giancana's daughter Antoinette who revealed this information in the book *Mafia Princess*.) Because of Giancana's suspected connection with the lodge at that time, the justice department kept tabs on the place. A taped conversation in December 1961 between Giancana and Roselli made clear Giancana's interest in Cal-Neva, and revealed that Sinatra was working in Giancana's behalf to persuade President John F. Kennedy and his family—namely, Robert Kennedy—to stop harassing Giancana.

"Did you go to [Lucky] Luciano's home?" Roselli asked Giancana.

"No."

"Oh, that's a hell of a place! A real nice home. He's a real nice guy."

"I couldn't get out of that country fast enough," Giancana snorted, referring to Italy, where Luciano had been deported.

"Skinny called me," Roselli said after a moment, "and said get hold of the guy, he wants to see you." Skinny was Paul D'Amato, an ex-mobster who ran Cal-Neva.

"Who was [the guy]?"

"Frank [Sinatra]. You know. So the first week I didn't see him. [Then] I saw him. 'Hello, how are you,' and that's all. After his wife left, he sent for me. . . . 'Now,' I said, 'Frank, I don't want to bother you.' He said, 'I want you to bunk with me. . . . Will you do that?' he says. 'Bunk with me?' I says. 'All right.' So he says, 'When are you going home?' I says, 'Today.' So he says, 'Cancel out. I want you to come to my home.' I says, 'That'll be fine with me.' So he was real nice to me and offered me some money. I threw it back at him."

The conversation at this point becomes confusing and difficult to follow. However, the idea was for Sinatra to request that the attorney general stop leaning on Giancana. Antoinette Giancana wrote that the tape "described efforts Sinatra made on behalf of my father to have the family of President John F. Kennedy ease the harassment of Sam."

Sinatra then asked Roselli if Giancana was still seeing Phyllis McGuire. Roselli said he thought so. Sinatra was dubious about the association. As Roselli told Giancana:

"He figures they can always find you through her."

"What am I supposed to do?" Giancana asked. "If I didn't have her—"

"—they'd follow the next girl." The FBI, of course.

"In other words, I should stick my head in the sand with my ass in the air. Is that it? Or I shouldn't go no place?"

"Between you and I, Frank saw Joe Kennedy three different times. He called him three times. . . . Joe Kennedy, the father."

"Called who?"

"Called Frank. So maybe he's starting to see the light. You're friends. He's got it in his head that they're not faithful to him. That's what I'm trying to get in his head."

"In other words, then, the donation that was

made." He meant the campaign contribution to John F. Kennedy's primary fight.

"That's what I was talking about."

"Had to pay for it, regardless."

"That's what made the issue with him. Nothing deliberate, take it back."

"In other words, if I even get a speeding ticket, none of these [bastards] would know me?"

"You told that right, buddy. And I'm for you a hundred percent for that—"

"They just worry about themselves and keep themselves clean, take the heat off of them."

"Sam, I think you got to start, you got to start giving them orders. 'This is it, Frank.' That's how you got to start."

"No, I let him get his own."

"He says, 'I'll put you on the payroll.' He says, 'I'll put you in the Cal-Neva and I'll open up a swinging bar. The boys will bankroll it and, if you can't, come to me.' I told him, 'I'm going to tell Sam everything.'"

Shortly after that, Giancana muttered, "I'm getting sick and tired of this."

"Aren't you going to be tied up with Cal-Neva?"

"Who gives a [shit] about Cal-Neva? [Fuck] him. Don't worry about it. I'm going to get my money out of there and I'm going to wind up with half of the joint with *no* money. It's not going to make any difference."

"If you do that, please send me there, will you? To look out for you?"

Apparently, shortly after that conversation, Giancana ordered one of his men to contact the government's agents, requesting a meeting between Giancana and the attorney general. Giancana wanted the FBI to ease up its surveillance on him. The agents reported that Giancana's man told them:

"Moe says that if Kennedy wants to talk, he should get in touch with Frank Sinatra to set it up." Robert Kennedy not only ignored this request but carried a copy of the report with him to the president.

It was shortly after this incident that the president revised his West Coast itinerary and stayed at Bing Crosby's place in Palm Springs rather than at Frank Sinatra's.

In the summer of 1962, Sinatra became interested in a cocktail waitress at the Cal-Neva. She was married to a local deputy sheriff, but this didn't deter the singer. The FBI report said that he made "improper advances" to her.

The deputy sheriff approached Sinatra and ordered him to leave his wife alone. The singer ignored the challenge and continued his activities. Then, toward the end of June, the deputy finally approached Sinatra inside the casino and punched him in the face. Sinatra sustained injuries to his mouth and had to cancel his singing engagement.

The FBI later linked Sinatra and Giancana in a report dated November 27, 1962. "Frank Sinatra and Eddie Fisher, accompanied by Sam Giancana, recently flew from Los Angeles, California, to Reno, Nevada, en route to Lake Tahoe, Nevada, in Frank Sinatra's private plane," the report stated. Although the Nevada State Gaming Control Board would have been interested in this fact—Giancana was one of eleven criminal figures blacklisted in the state of Nevada and excluded from appearance at the lodge—the government agents did not pass on the information.

But the fat was really in the fire the next sum-

mer when Giancana appeared once again at Tahoe—
and got caught. At this time Giancana's girlfriend
was still Phyllis McGuire of the McGuire singing
trio. The FBI had discovered in October 1963 that
Giancana was trying to persuade Frank Sinatra to
give Phyllis McGuire a role in the Sinatra film
Come Blow Your Horn. It was to help McGuire get
this part that Giancana arrived at the Cal-Neva
ostensibly to attend the opening of the McGuire
Sisters' ten-day stint at the hostelry's Celebrity
Room. Giancana was well aware that he was barred
from attendance at Cal-Neva. To avoid being seen,
he kept a very low profile, living in Phyllis McGuire's
cottage on the shore of Lake Tahoe.

This time agents of the Nevada State Gaming
Control Board spotted him. They immediately informed Sinatra that he had broken the law by allowing Giancana to frequent the casino. It was his
duty, they pointed out, once he had identified a
known criminal figure, to bar him from the casino.
The gaming control board's "black list," which he
had in his possession, clearly included Giancana.

The situation was exacerbated when Giancana
got into an argument with one of McGuire's staff
members in the Cal-Neva bar and gave him a punch
in the face. A Cal-Neva employee who was witness
to the fracas was ordered by the control board to
attend its hearings and testify against Giancana.
However, the employee mysteriously failed to appear
at the hearing. The board accused Sinatra of having something to do with the witness's failure to
appear.

It did not end there. Sinatra telephoned the chairman of the control board, a man named Edward A.
Olsen, and invited him up to the lodge for dinner.

"We can talk about this thing." Olsen told Sinatra he felt that such a conversation was inappropriate, since his board was investigating the hotel. Nevertheless, Sinatra kept insisting.

"I kept refusing," Olsen said. "The more I refused, the madder he got, until he seemed almost hysterical. He used the foulest language I ever heard in my life."

Finally Sinatra declared that if Olsen would not come to see him to talk, he would never talk to *anyone* from the board.

By now Olsen was angry himself. "If we want to talk to you, we will subpoena you."

"You subpoena me," Sinatra said, "and you're going to get a big, fat, fucking surprise."

"It was clear to me he meant that as a threat," Olsen said.

Now Paul D'Amato, Cal-Neva's manager, got into the act. When two agents of the gaming board entered the place to make a routine inspection, he slipped two $100 bills to them—or tried to. The agents returned the money and reported the bribe. Governor Grant Sawyer of Nevada suddenly began getting phone calls from people who wanted to make big contributions to his upcoming campaign for reelection. "I told them that the rules were made for everyone, including Mr. Sinatra," he said.

In spite of all this action in the wings, the state gaming control board filed its report, charging that Sinatra had failed to carry out his "duties"; it also charged him with attempting to intimidate officials of the board.

"Giancana sojourned in Chalet 50 at the Cal-Neva Lodge at various times between July 17 and July 28, 1963, with the knowledge and consent of the licensee [Sinatra]."

The upshot of all this action was that the board ordered Sinatra's license revoked. Sinatra turned it in voluntarily and promised to divest himself of his interest in Cal-Neva and also his interest in the Sands Hotel in Las Vegas. They were worth at that time about three and a half million dollars.

Sometime later, on September 19, 1963, Giancana discussed with two unidentified associates a $3 million loan that Giancana had unsuccessfully tried to secure from Jimmy Hoffa and the Central States Teamsters pension fund. "In regard to this conversation," the FBI said, "it is believed that the request for the three-million-dollar loan was in connection with a request by Frank Sinatra for a similar amount for the purpose of renovating the Cal-Neva Lodge, supposedly owned by Sinatra but believed in actuality to be owned by Giancana."

Sinatra and Giancana had a falling out several years later. The reason seemed to be money. Johnny Roselli spoke about it to Los Angeles Mafia boss Jimmy Fratianno: "Jimmy, Frank and I are on the outs. Sinatra took Sam for a lot of money when he sold Cal-Neva. He's come across with some money, but don't worry. Sammy's going to get the rest."

Vis-à-vis the selling of Cal-Neva, Howard Hughes, the billionaire recluse, was approached in 1967 by Sinatra's group as a potential buyer. Hughes turned down the offer and instead purchased the Sands in Las Vegas. This infuriated Sinatra, who needed the money from the Cal-Neva sale, and who felt that the Sands was *his* turf—not Howard Hughes's. It was shortly after this that, as the media had it, "the King erupted."

Sinatra's "eruption" began when he failed to appear for a one-month engagement at the Sands shortly after Hughes bought it. He finally arrived, seven days late, but was infuriated to discover when he approached the gaming tables that his gambling credit had been ordered cut off by Carl Cohen, the casino manager. Sinatra already owed about $500,000. But still, it was a kick in the face for the man who considered the grounds his own private club. "I built this hotel from a sand pile and before I'm through, that is what it will be again!" he reportedly said.

Although the story has become confused through many retellings, Sinatra apparently tried without success to confront Cohen directly, and then, thwarted, began his tactical operations against Cohen and Sands by lighting a fire in his private suite and trying to torch the place. After this attempt failed, he went downstairs and somehow got hold of an electric baggage cart. He drove this out into the swimming pool and began knocking the outdoor furniture into the pool. With most of the furniture dumped, he found a huge concrete ashtray and pushed it through a plate-glass window. A security guard who was trying to stop him was injured in the crash.

Now Sinatra turned his attention again to Cohen. Hurling all his familiar obscenities, he rushed to the hotel's telephone room on the second floor. When the telephone operators would not connect him with his nemesis, he yanked out all the switchboard jacks and disconnected the trunk lines—while the wide-eyed operators watched.

He wasn't through by a long shot. Now thoroughly aroused, he took umbrage once again at the fact that his credit had been cut off and approached the casino. He buttonholed people he didn't even know and told them that his credit had been cut off. *His* credit! It was all Howard Hughes's fault. Howard Hughes had cut him off and had no right to. Howard Hughes was loaded with money. As Sinatra saw it, it was Howard Hughes's *duty* to pay Sinatra because it was Sinatra and his friends who had made the Sands famous and profitable in the first place.

He became infuriated with the pit boss who refused to let him play. "I'm going to break both your legs!" he cried at the employee.

By now he was heading for the Garden Room restaurant, still in search of Cohen. There he found his quarry, seated at a table. When Sinatra saw him, he gave a cry of triumph and rushed into the room. There he upset the table and threw it on top of Cohen. Cohen was pushed to the floor.

A good-natured, gray-haired man about Sinatra's age, Cohen weighed in at a good 250 pounds. He was not about to let himself be downed in this manner. He pushed the table off himself, and jumped up. He then swung at Sinatra, and hit him in the mouth. Blood started to flow from Sinatra's mouth, and he was beside himself with rage. Now he began yelling at Cohen for punching him. Sinatra turned around and seized the nearest thing at hand. It was a chair. He threw it at Cohen, missed, but hit a security guard, and opened a cut in the man's head.

Robert Maheu, a former FBI and CIA agent with underworld connections and at that time Howard Hughes's right-hand man, later wrote a detailed report of Sinatra's doings and the imbroglio that ensued: "At six A.M. today, Sinatra appeared at the Sands, made one hell of a scene and insisted on seeing Carl Cohen. He threatened to kill anyone who got in his way, used vile language, and said he would beat up the telephone operators if they did not connect him with Cohen, etc.

"In an effort to calm the situation, Carl agreed to meet him. Sinatra called Cohen every dirty name in the book, said he was going to kill him, pushed a table over on Carl, picked up a chair and attempted to hit Carl over the head. Carl ducked, took a pass at Sinatra and floored him. I understand Frank has a broken tooth." At the end of the fracas, Sinatra confronted Maheu and canceled his engagement at the Sands Hotel.

In fact, Sinatra had not one broken tooth, but two. He flew in his dentist, Dr. A. B. Weinstein, from New York, and flew himself to Los Angeles to get his teeth recapped.

"They wouldn't give me any credit in the casino," Sinatra explained to the press, "and I quit." He said he had simply walked across the way and signed on at Caesars Palace, the Sands's most formidable rival.

This tactic did not sit well with Howard Hughes.

"I don't intend to take this lying down," Hughes said, intimating that Caesars Palace had stolen Sinatra away from him to profit from his name. "Sinatra made three pictures for me at RKO. I know him backward and frontward. All actors are a little crazy. But I don't intend the Caesars group making us look weak and stupid."

More than anything, Hughes was incensed at losing Sinatra to his toughest rival. He wanted Sinatra at the Sands. He huddled with Maheu and they came up with a scheme to get their big attraction back. It was Hughes's idea to play on Sinatra's loyalty and sentimentality. Maheu was instructed to say something along these lines: "Howard doesn't know if you remember the time when you were friends. But he remembers—it was back in the days when you were flying a Bonanza, one of the first ones on the Coast. Anyway, he remembers, and when he heard of the recent events, he was distressed beyond measure."

(Listen to those soaring violins!)

"However, he was hesitant to inject himself between you and Cohen, since you had been close friends for such a very long time. He even remembers (or thinks he remembers) you introducing Sammy Davis, Jr., to the public for the first time from the stage of the Sands."

(Now very sincere orchestral music, *tutti*.)

"Anyway, returning to recent events, the story that was related to him was so fantastic it seemed as if it could only have occurred in a nightmare, not in reality."

And to conclude this scenario, Hughes instructed Maheu: "Please tell Frank that the only way I know to show that the recent events do not in any way reflect my feelings or wishes is to suggest that he visit the Sands or the Desert Inn and ask for $500,000 or $1,000,000 in chips and see what results he gets. I think he will find that he is not even asked to sign the marker."

Sinatra refused the offer. In point of fact, Hughes had been right when he intimated that Sinatra was trying to manufacture some excuse to leave the Sands. It developed that Sinatra had been negotiating with Caesars Palace for two months and had, indeed, already signed up before the big trash job at the Sands.

There was still more. Cohen had cut off Sinatra's credit because he was running up huge tabs at the time he was actually planning to leave for Caesars Palace. And Cohen correctly suspected that Sinatra might be hard up for cash at the time. Unknown to the public, Sinatra had been frantically trying to unload Cal-Neva Lodge to the Hughes interests.

And behind the scenes there was always Sam Giancana leaning on him for *his* money.

Nor was that the end of it. At the same time that the Caesars Palace people were signing up Sinatra, they were in the act of purchasing Cal-Neva from Sinatra, thus letting him off the financial hook. Sinatra was once and for all not the Sicilian he would like the myth to portray, with a memory for snubs and insults, but rather the tough-minded businessman to whom financial matters were always more important than personal ones.

Sinatra's publicists smoothed everything over for the media in a typical release. "I have admired and respected Howard Hughes for many years," the puff said, "and regret that my decision to accept the offer of Caesars Palace comes so soon after his acquisition of the Sands."

Uh-huh.

The media had a field day with the brouhaha. They had their own view of it. In their eyes, Sinatra had been kicked out of the Sands by Hughes because of their mutual and deep-felt jealousies over Ava Gardner and Lana Turner—both of whom, each felt, preferred the other to himself.

The joke that made the rounds in Vegas was that, when informed of Frank's departure from the Sands, Hughs responded, "Frank who?"

Caesars Palace was user-friendly to Sinatra—at least for two or three years. He loved to gamble on credit—and Caesars had his tab up to almost a million dollars by September 6, 1970. It was on this day that everything came apart for Sinatra at Caesars.

Again, it was an early-morning blowup. Sinatra and his friends were spending freely in the casino at about five A.M. after an all-night party, but Sinatra was playing on credit. In fact, he was working a game in which the $8,000 house limit had been doubled. At this point Sanford Waterman, the hotel's executive vice-president, was informed that Sinatra was way over the limit. Waterman came out of his suite and confronted Sinatra. As politely as possible, he told Sinatra that he could no longer draw on his credit.

Seated at the table, Sinatra was fingering a pile of chips in his hand as he pondered over Waterman's ukase and, abruptly, with no warning, turned and threw the whole stack of chips into the man's face, leaped up out of his chair, and grasped Waterman by the throat as if to throttle him.

The casino's security guards, seeing their boss in the grip of the feisty entertainer, immediately tried to intercede, grabbing Sinatra quickly to pull him off. But Sinatra's own bodyguards intervened and started scrapping with the security men. A loud fracas ensued, with everybody swinging fists and shouting.

Then Waterman pulled a handgun. This was enough to cool even Sinatra. He let go of Waterman's throat. His face tightened. "This gun shit went out twenty years ago!" he snapped in the manner of a Golden Age movie gangster. Then he looked around disdainfully and snapped his fingers. "I'm leaving. Is anybody leaving with me?"

As he left the room the door—by accident or intent—closed on his hand. Angrily Sinatra faced

the crowd in the gaming room. "The mob will take
care of you!" he was reported to have said.

Authorities arrested Waterman for assault with
a deadly weapon. District Attorney George Franklin took charge of the investigation, and when he
found bruises on Waterman's throat that could only
have been made by somebody's fingers, he released
him. Then Franklin announced to the press that his
office was going to look into Sinatra's background.
His men, he said, were going to find out "who owns
the nightclubs where [Sinatra] sang in his early
days, who started him on his way, and about his
friendship with the underworld."

The sheriff of Las Vegas, Ralph Lamb, stated
publicly that he was tired of Sinatra and his
actions—"intimidating waiters, starting fires," and
so on. "He gets away with too much," he said. "He's
through picking on little people in this town. Why
the owners of the hotels put up with this is what I
plan to find out." He added, "If he gives me any
trouble, he's going to jail."

Sinatra stayed away for a while, but soon enough
he was back. On his return, Caesars Palace initiated a new policy for protecting Frank Sinatra and
for protecting itself against the Sinatra presence.
This policy included the addition of twenty-five extra security guards, all heavily armed, whenever
Sinatra was in residence.

The appearance of Sinatra would mean a huge
entourage of support troops. There would be the
district attorney's men, the hotel's extra security
forces, and Sinatra's own muscle detail. The Sinatra
guards wore black opaque sunglasses, stony expres-
sions, and a bulge under the left armpit. No one
could come within thirty feet of the entertainer,

unless he specifically asked to have that person approach within the charmed circle. When Sinatra came down for dinner or a drink with friends or acquaintances, there would be an armed guard behind each chair at the table or bar, standing in the attitude of a palace guard, arms akimbo, giving everyone within eyeball range the evil eye.

But at least the temper explosions seemed to have become fewer and farther between.

Although Sinatra performed at the Villa Venice in Wheeling, Illinois, he did not own it. An FBI report dated December 14, 1962, stated that "Sam Giancana is definitely the owner of the Villa Venice, and has spent many hours overseeing the remodeling operation of the Villa Venice during the past several weeks. Giancana is referred to at the Villa Venice as 'Mr. Flood.'"

According to the FBI, an unidentified source "advised in September 1962 that the Villa Venice is definitely an operation of the Chicago criminal organization headed by Samuel Giancana. . . . Sinatra made the arrangement for Giancana concerning the appearance of Eddie Fisher for the opening act commencing with October 31, 1962."

At the behest of Attorney General Robert Kennedy the FBI then recorded a conversation between Giancana and another person on September 13, 1962, at the Armory Lounge in Chicago. The person's identity was withheld.

"We'll open up the thirty-first and then you'll work a weekend. Then—"

"Frank [Sinatra] and Dean [Martin] and, uh, Sammy [Davis, Jr.]. Frank, uh, Debbie Reynolds—"

"Eddie Fisher comes in first," Giancana said. "And

that's all taken care of. I mean, the living quarters. You know that Eddie Fisher? There's a guy with a broken heart. He can leave the seventh, or whenever his week is up. All you got to do is call Eddie and tell him to come in. Get Frank. Then we're going to do a show around Debbie Reynolds. There's nothing yet." Later on in the recording, Giancana griped about Sinatra. "That Frank, he wants more money, he wants this, he wants that, he wants more girls, he wants ... I don't need that or him. I broke my [ass] when I was talking to him in New York."

In 1962, Sinatra told the FBI he had performed at the Villa Venice only out of friendship for Leo Olsen, the front owner of the nightclub. He could not recall meeting Giancana at the Villa Venice. But the media knew. On December 1, 1962, the *Chicago Tribune* published a story that the illegal casino was created "by the syndicate chief, Momo Salvatore (Moe) Giancana, to tap the bankrolls of patrons drawn to the Villa Venice by the nightclub act of Frank Sinatra, Sammy Davis, Jr., and Dean Martin.

"The betting den began full-blast operations when Sinatra and his group opened at the Villa Venice, it was learned.

"A host of gangsters were on hand for Sinatra's first night, investigators said. Among them were Giancana, Willie (Potatoes) Daddano, Marshall Caifano, Jimmy (the Monk) Allegretti, and Flex (Milwaukee Phil) Alderiso.

"Sinatra's gangland fans from other cities appeared too, authorities disclosed. The Florida contingent was led by Joe Fischetti, from Miami. A delegation of Wisconsin gangsters, including Jim DeGeorge, occupied a ringside table."

SINATRA: THE MAN AND THE MYTH

* * *

The fact that Sinatra had always associated with
mobsters never seemed to matter to any of the
women he was squiring around. In 1976 Jimmy
Fratianno met with Sinatra at the 21 Club in New
York City. Rona Barrett, the television and newspaper gossip columnist, had left the club only moments before when she learned that Sinatra would
arrive shortly. They had been feuding for years.
Sinatra hated her and made no bones about his
feelings. After a while Sinatra recognized Jackie
Onassis sitting at another table.

"Look at her," he told Fratianno in a low voice.
"She's been gunning me all night."

Fratianno looked in her direction, but at that moment Jackie Onassis turned her gaze away from
them and toward her escort. Fratianno went to sit
with Jilly Rizzo and Tommy Marson at another
table. They began to discuss Sinatra and Jackie
Onassis. "Have you noticed how Jackie's been gunning Frank?" Fratianno observed.

"You kidding?" Rizzo responded. "She can't take
her eyes off him. She and Frank were going at it
pretty hot and heavy for a while. She was nuts
about him, but Frank never stuck to nobody very
long in them days."

There was more talk.

"See," Rizzo went on, "Frank says that Jackie
wanted to marry him, but he dropped her like a hot
potato. To him she's just another broad, right? He's
already had what he wanted, right, so what's he
going to do with her now that she wants to get
married? You know what I mean? He said, 'See you
later, baby, bye-bye.' "

Fratianno once recalled an incident involving Sinatra and Benny Macri, a union organizer. "I ran into them at the Desert Inn," Fratianno said. "Frank wants to go see his cousin, Ray Sinatra, who's playing at some other joint. I'd just gotten my new Caddy and Frank gets behind the wheel, he wants to drive that motherfucker. So he starts backing up at a hundred miles an hour and nearly clips that sheriff, Glen Jones. Well, shit, Frank jumps out of the car and starts calling Jones a motherfucker, and everything. That fucking Sinatra's crazy, you know. I say, 'Frank, leave it alone.'

"This whole time Jones's not saying a word. He can't figure out what's happening. Anyway, we leave, but I'm thinking about Jones. I make excuses and I come right back to the [Desert Inn] and Jones is sitting in the cocktail lounge. I says, 'Glen, I'm sorry, but this fucking Sinatra's nuts.' "

★ 11 ★

September Song

The 1960s were an unusual decade in American social history, marked by an intensification of the country's fetish for youth. And in the White House, the Kennedys had set the style for youth, for big money, for glamour, and for the newly styled Beautiful People.

Most of Frank Sinatra's faithful were now middle-aged—as he himself was. And they seemed to yearn for the youth they had left behind. Sinatra was one of the few who could do something about it; he knew he could regain his youth through one of the things he did best: romancing women. He chose what many considered at the time a strange object: Mia Farrow, who was thirty years younger than he and five years younger than his daughter Nancy, Jr. Mia was the daughter of actress Maureen O'Sullivan and director John Farrow.

Or did she choose him?

A product of the sixties, Mia was totally unlike Sinatra's other love objects: Ava Gardner, Lana Turner, or even his wife Nancy Sinatra. She was thin, intellectually tough, stubborn, and challenging. By the time she was ten years old she had been kicked out of two convent schools for refusing to accept the teaching of the nuns and priests.

When Maureen O'Sullivan heard that Sinatra was going to marry her daughter, she snapped, "Marry Mia? He should marry *me*!"

Sinatra was only four years younger than Mia's *mother*!

They met in October 1964 on the Twentieth Century–Fox set of *Von Ryan's Express,* a property that Sinatra had bought to star in. Mia Farrow was also working on the Fox lot, playing in the television serial *Peyton Place.*

One day she visited the set to see John Leyton, an English actor she had met. "I had some time off," she said later, "and I was fooling around the *Von Ryan's* set, climbing up in the rafters. I remember that Edward Mulhare was there, and Frank [Sinatra] was climbing out of one of the freight cars." Mia was embarrassed, and wanted to get out of their way. She found Leyton, and he let her ride the motorcycles and cars being used.

"I saw Frank again, and it got to be 'Hello, Mr. Sinatra.' " Then, "He asked me to a screening of one of his pictures, and of course I went. I liked him instantly. He rings true. He *is* what he is."

Hollywood columnist Sheila Graham saw what was going on and reported that Mia Farrow was talking on the telephone with Frank Sinatra on the set of *Peyton Place.* But everybody else simply fobbed it off as a casual thing. These talks soon grew into weekends spent down at Sinatra's Palm Springs place. They would eat at Ruby's during these desert weekends, not making any public appearance in Los Angeles until a charity luncheon in 1965.

Now that it was out in the open all the comics took up the May-September theme. Jack E. Leonard said he respected Sinatra for choosing Mia Farrow because she didn't smoke or drink. "She's still teething," he said. Dean Martin told Sinatra that he had a case of Scotch in his house that was older than Mia Farrow.

In July 1965 it was announced in the gossip columns that Mia Farrow was going to be Frank Sinatra's companion on a month-long cruise, chaperoned by solid members of the Hollywood Establishment—including Rosalind Russell and her husband, and Claudette Colbert and her husband. The writers of *Peyton Place* were putting the character played by Mia Farrow into a six-week coma to bridge the gap.

The first week in August the *Southern Breeze*, a 168-foot yacht chartered by Sinatra at $2,000 a day, sailed out of Newport, Rhode Island. Soon she anchored and Sinatra stepped ashore to visit the ailing Joseph Kennedy. That same afternoon a woman in white sneakers, white pants, black sweater, and white kerchief boarded the yacht with the returnees—and suddenly everybody was agog.

Headline on the *New York Daily News*:

JACKIE SEES FRANKIE AND HIS DREAMBOAT

"I saw this girl in a black sweater. It looked like Jacqueline Kennedy," said Associated Press photographer J. Walter Green later in some embarrassment. "I watched the black sweater get out of the boat, black sweater go up the ladder, black sweater greet Sinatra."

Turned out "Jackie" was really Patricia Lawford.

That wasn't the only event during the cruise. On August 10, two crewmen who had missed the last launch to the yacht tried to make it out in a hired dinghy. It capsized, and one man drowned. He had given the only life preserver to his fellow crew member, who could not swim. The drowned man had been married less than a year. His widow and her family paid a visit to the *Southern Breeze*. Later, the widow's father told the press: "I haven't heard from Sinatra, and I don't care if we ever do. We were on his boat and apparently he didn't see fit to offer his condolence."

Then, just shortly after he had finished making a record album titled *September of My Years,* Sinatra and Mia Farrow publicly stated to friends and associates in New York that Frank would be flying to London the next day to go to work for a short time.

The two of them were arm in arm, and both seemed relaxed. At three-fifteen in the morning, they left, Frank saying, "See you in about two months."

Instead of flying to London, Sinatra climbed aboard his private jet and flew to Las Vegas and the Sands Hotel where he met Mia. She had gone first to Los Angeles and then come back to Vegas. In Jack Entratter's suite at the Sands they were married privately on July 19, 1966; at least, no members of either the bride or the groom's family was present. "I think we handled that pretty good," he bragged.

He was fifty-one, she was twenty-one. She cut her hair short and wore pants. She opposed the Vietnam War. "He digs her brain," Sinatra's friends explained. But nobody really believed this.

Besides, the question really was: what did she see in him? Was it the romantic aura that had surrounded him for years? Was it his wealth and power? It certainly was *not* his friends. Sometime later she was quoted as saying: "All they know how to do is tell dirty stories, break furniture, pinch waitresses' asses and bet on the horses."

The Sinatras rented a house in Bel Air that had belonged to Buddy Adler. And then, quite predictably, it all cooled down. Sinatra was moody. Mia was moody. Mia, like her mother Maureen, had a guru with whom she could meditate. Mia spent hours meditating. Sinatra couldn't care less about Mia's guru and what *he* thought. He wanted to get out on the town and have fun with his friends and entourage.

Sinatra had bought a new movie property called *The Detective* he was going to film. He wanted his wife to star in it with him. Her agent wanted her to do *Rosemary's Baby*. The argument escalated. Sinatra wanted a dramatic husband-and-wife combo along the lines of Richard Burton and Elizabeth Taylor. Mia couldn't dig that. After numerous spats they met in Miami Beach and talked it over. And after that it was indeed done with. Mia hid out in Bel Air, where she could not be reached.

In January 1968 after the efforts of many friends to get the pair of them together again, Mia flew to India for a month of meditation with the Maharishi Mahesh Yogi, the guru who had been connected to the Beatles and the Rolling Stones.

When she returned, she and Sinatra tried to get back together, but the separation had gone on too long. In August 1968 it was all over.

That was the story as the public saw it through the media. But Sinatra had not changed his ways of living at all. If anything, he was swinging as much as he ever had—with other women of all temperaments, shapes, and sizes.

This was during the years he was still working for the Sands Hotel in Las Vegas. According to Ed Reid and Ovid Demaris, the staff of the Sands had always feared him. Even when he was absent from the place, his tape-recorded voice remained to haunt them, echoing through the hallways and corridors. Sinatra ordered the first steam room in Vegas to be built in the Sands for his particular use. It cost the management $40,000 and was nicknamed the "Clubhouse of the Clan." Those were the days when the Clan—or most of it—was still functioning.

The staff of the Sands may have feared and loathed Sinatra, but the show girls loved him. One of the most popular in Vegas was Sheika "Yellowbird" Moisha, who fell in love with Sinatra. But she was always falling in love. She had been seen with a number of men, including such luminaries as Cary Grant and Ricky Nelson. Yellowbird had been a big hit at El Rancho before it burned to the ground. Everyone who came to see her there loved her yellow feathery costume—for which she was aptly nicknamed. Her boss, Beldon Katleman, preferred her to all of his other show girls—until she met Sinatra and fell for him.

There was a standing rule at El Rancho that show girls had to stay around the casino between shows and after the last show at two-thirty in the morning. That was to entice customers to remain after hours. Yellowbird started breaking the rules. She would sneak out between shows to go to the Sands to watch Sinatra perform.

Katleman hated Sinatra and the Sands. When he found out about Yellowbird's actions, he became incensed. He read her the riot act and told her that if she continued to sneak out of El Rancho between shows he would fire her.

Yellowbird quit so she could be with Sinatra. He assured her that she had nothing to worry about even if she had been fired. He would provide for her.

In reality, Sinatra was not the only love of Yellowbird's life. She also hung out at the Tail o' the Pup and Maxine's, two taverns that were patronized by lesbians.

But she was only one of many in Sinatra's stable. In fact women were only a part of his nightlife—as he had always lived it. He loved to cruise around town—wherever he was—with his entourage of friends and partisans. He exerted a tremendous charm on some people; from others he elicited tremendous fear and loathing.

Gay Talese wrote about him for *Esquire* magazine in 1966, detailing an encounter that seemed to bring the myth of Sinatra into focus. In a private club in Beverly Hills, Sinatra and his entourage were in the pool room with a group of younger men—one of them a "little guy, very quick of movement, who had a sharp profile, pale blue eyes, blondish hair, and squared eyeglasses." He wore game-warden boots, which, for some reason, bothered Sinatra. Talese knew the booted patron of the club: he was Harlan Ellison, a writer who had written the screenplay for the movie *The Oscar*.

"Hey," Sinatra yelled in that edged voice of his. "Those Italian boots?"

"No."

"Spanish?"

"No."

"Are they *English* boots?"

Ellison was getting tired of this. "I dunno, man."

The pool room quieted down. Tension grew. Even the noise of the balls stopped. Sinatra moved toward Ellison with a sinister arrogance.

"You expecting a . . . *storm?*"

Ellison protested, moving away from Sinatra nervously.

"I don't like the way you're dressed," Sinatra snapped.

"I dress to suit myself," Ellison responded.

Ellison's friends tried to get him out of the pool room, but he was disturbed now, and wanted to make his stand.

"What do you do?" Sinatra asked.

"I'm a plumber," Ellison answered.

One of Ellison's friends broke in: "He wrote *The Oscar*."

Sinatra nodded. "Oh, yeah. Well, I've seen it, and it's a piece of crap."

Ellison straightened up. "That's strange, because they haven't even released it yet."

"Well, I've seen it, and it's a piece of crap!"

One of Sinatra's entourage now stepped in and tried to persuade Ellison to leave the pool room.

Sinatra protested. "Can't you see I'm talking to this guy?"

A few more verbal jabs were exchanged, and finally Ellison left the pool room with his friends. News of the argument, and Sinatra's participation, had spread through the club. Word was that the manager of

the club had heard about it and had driven home.
And so the assistant manager appeared. Sinatra
turned to him. "I don't want anybody in here without coats and ties."

Talese wrote: "It seemed that Sinatra was only
half-serious, perhaps just reacting out of sheer bore-
dom or inner despair."

Talese did not mention the fact that Sinatra played
himself in a cameo bit in *The Oscar* and may well
have known who Ellison was before he began to
bait him. Or was it all a typical rib of Sinatra's?

Whatever, Talese's profile was a revealing one of
the Sinatra of the sixties—a mixture of decency and
arrogance, a lot of clout with nowhere to go, nerve
endings waiting for a new thrill of some kind.

In 1967, Sinatra made a recording called "Some-
thin' Stupid" with his daughter Nancy. It climbed
to Number One in both the United States and Great
Britain. In the same year, of course, he switched
from the Sands to Caesars Palace. Later, in 1969,
he recorded "My Way," now generally considered
a perfect reflection of his personality and his life-
style.

Politically, Sinatra had been simmering ever since
the Kennedys had snubbed him in 1962. His Sicilian blood would not let that wound heal. As his
mother had once said about him: "My son is like
me. You cross him, he never forgets." And in 1968,
he found a way to get back at Robert Kennedy, who
was making the run for the presidency. Sinatra
announced his support for Hubert Humphrey in the
California primary against Robert Kennedy. "Bobby's just not qualified to be president," he told
reporters.

Kennedy, of course, was assassinated shortly after the California win over Humphrey. Whether or not that was a deciding factor, Sinatra quit the campaign and did not even support Humphrey publicly.

It was not surprising that by now he had managed to develop a physical problem—however slight—and seemed quite a bit bothered by it. Called Dupuytren's Contracture, the ailment caused a distortion of the palm and fingers of his right hand—the "microphone" hand. In 1970 he had an operation to correct the condition, which was somewhat alleviated, but not totally cured.

In a way, it seemed to be time to—well, on March 21, 1971, he went public with the following statement: "I wish to announce, effective immediately, my retirement from the entertainment world and public life." He elaborated on his "great and good fortune" in the three decades of his career, but noted that he needed a pause for a little self-examination, reflection, and reading. And it ended with the following: "This seems a proper time to take that breather."

And so on June 14, 1971, Sinatra made his farewell apperance at the Los Angeles Music Center, with tickets priced at $250 each and the profits going to the Motion Picture and Television Relief Fund.

As Sinatra got into his tuxedo jacket and started for the wings, Don Rickles called out to the crowd of stars backstage: "Somebody help the old man on with his coat. Make way for the old-timer. Help him go out in a blaze of glory. Remember, Frank, pity!" Rosalind Russell, an old friend, was more formal in her introduction of Sinatra. "It's time to put back the Kleenex and stifle the sob, for we still have the man, we still have the blue eyes, those wonderful blue eyes, that smile, for one last time we have the man, the greatest entertainer of the twentieth century."

And he sang. And when he was through, doing "That's Life," and finally "Angel Eyes"—"It's a saloon song and I've been a saloon singer"—he staged his finale.

In the middle of the song, he lit a cigarette, exhaled the smoke in a billowing cloud around him. And at the last line of the song, he changed the words: "Excuse me while I disappear."

The spot blinked out.

He was gone.

It was all very show-biz and right down Sinatra's alley. It took someone like John Rockwell, the *New York Times* music critic, to view this "retirement" from a slightly different perspective. "The principal activity of his retirement years was his political shift from left to right," he wrote.

That was coming—but it was actually somewhat slow in arriving. There were reasons. One of the reasons occurred in July 1972. In that month Sinatra was summoned before the House Select Committee on Crime, to answer questions raised by Joe (the Baron) Barboza, a convicted felon. Barboza had testified two months earlier that Sinatra had invested in two multi-million-dollar hotels as a front for reputed New England Mafia boss Raymond Patriarca and Gaetano (Three-Fingers Brown) Luchese, a New York family *capo*.

According to Barboza, Sinatra and had taken a

piece of the ill-fated Berkshire Downs racetrack in Massachusetts, in which Patriarca was said to have sunk $215,000.

In court, Sinatra denied that he had ever even heard Patriarca's name. He said, in addition, that he had no idea who else had interests in the Berkshire track. As for the $55,000 he was supposed to have put into the operation, he said he had been planning to invest in it but had pulled out after track officials put his name on the operation as a director without his permission.

Did he have business dealings with the late Gaetano Luchese in New York? Sinatra said that he had had no business dealing with him. He did admit, though, that he had met him "two or three times."

Did he know that Luchese was a racketeer? "That's his problem, not mine!" Sinatra snapped. "Let's dispense with that kind of question." It was, as *Time* magazine pointed out, "a bravura performance for a man who has in the past stoutly defended his right to associate with questionable characters."

Patriarca himself was brought up from Atlanta Federal Prison where he was serving a ten-year sentence for conspiracy to murder. He denied knowing Sinatra. "The only place I've seen him is on television," he told his questioners. To most of the questions asked him, he pleaded the Fifth Amendment, admitting, however, that he liked *The Godfather*. "In my opinion, it was a good book. People like to read that."

There was a great deal more to this episode than Sinatra's sparring match with the Washington politicians. The motivation of the hearings was apparently an investigation into Sinatra's mob ties. And it was all the more interesting because John Tunney—an old Kennedy friend and a California politician for whom Sinatra had raised $160,000 when he was running for office—was the head of the committee!

Were the Kennedys still reaching out to haunt him all the way from the grave?

Once again Sinatra went public—this time about his political thinking. For his forum he chose the Op-Ed page of the *New York Times,* and on July 24, 1972, six days after the hearing, he wrote about his new outlook on government and the people. He no longer believed that government was the savior of the people. He saw the rights of private citizens now in conflict with certain aspects of government. He mentioned Joseph McCarthy, and "star chambers," and the destruction of reputations and characters by innuendo and gossip. "In my case, a convicted murderer was allowed to throw my name around with abandon, while the TV cameras rolled on." His privacy, he said, had been "robbed" from him. "I was being forced to defend myself in a place that was not even a court of law." If it could happen to him, it could happen to anyone. What was the answer?

The answer for Frank Sinatra was to become a Republican and vote for Ronald Reagan—who, coincidentally, happened to be running for office that year in California. Nationally, of course, Richard Nixon was running for president with Spiro Agnew on the same ticket for vice-president.

No one ever was very clear exactly when and where Sinatra and Agnew first met, but Maxine Cheshire wrote that it probably occurred at a political rally in California in 1971 when Governor Ronald Reagan introduced the two of them.

After that, Agnew was a constant guest at the Sinatra compound—more so after Sinatra's retirement. In 1971, Agnew and his family spent Easter, Thanksgiving, and New Year's Eve with Sinatra.

And with the Nixon–Agnew team triumphant in 1972, Sinatra quietly went to work. He continued and intensified his friendship with Vice-President Spiro Agnew, and the two were seen constantly together playing golf and attending parties in Palm Springs. Naturally enough, Agnew introduced Sinatra to the president, and he became persona grata in the highest of political circles. Sinatra now found himself becoming more newsworthy than ever—as a friend of the powerful rather than as an entertainer.

At that time he was going around with Barbara Marx, a former Las Vegas show girl and ex-wife of Zeppo Marx, the fourth Marx Brother. Maxine Cheshire discovered that Sinatra was involved with Barbara and did a column about his interest in her. "Reporters in Washington, as well as Hollywood, will be watching to see if Sinatra is accompanied here next month by Barbara Marx," she wrote, after explaining that Sinatra would be in Washington for a series of pre-inaugural parties. "The fortyish, tennis-playing Mrs. Marx, who has a college-age son, recently filed for divorce from comedian Zeppo Marx. She has attracted recent attention from political reporters who don't ordinarily keep up with movieland romances because her friendship with Sinatra has brought her into the tight little 'inside' group around Vice-President Spiro T. Agnew.

"With Sinatra, she flew here on Agnew's plane to accompany the Vice-President to the Apollo moonshot. And when Sinatra broke retirement—for one appearance only—to sing at an Agnew fund-raiser in Chicago last summer, she was there."

Cheshire held back on the hottest news she had: that Sinatra would soon marry Barbara Marx. The White House, however, was unhappy over another piece Cheshire had written for *Parade* magazine, reporting that Sinatra had introduced "two lovelies (Eva Gabor and Barbara Marx) to Agnew, who finds the Sinatra life-style most conducive to enjoyment."

"How do you think Mrs. Agnew feels when she reads something like this?" Spiro Agnew's then-press secretary Victor Gold asked her.

And that was the background for what happened at the Fairfax Hotel when Sinatra arrived the night before the inauguration, accompanied by Barbara Marx, for the gala party given for the Republican National Committee at the Jockey Club. In the hotel lobby, Maxine Cheshire approached Barbara Marx and introduced herself. "We've talked on the telephone," she explained.

Sinatra, at that point several feet away, whirled around and burst out in an absolute fury at the reporter:

"Get away from me, you scum!" he shouted. "Go home and take a bath! I don't want to talk to you!" he cried. "I'm getting out of here to get rid of the stench of Miss Cheshire."

About thirty astonished onlookers stared at the group. Sinatra turned and addressed them vehemently. "You know Miss Cheshire, don't you? That stench you smell is from her." His face turned redder and redder. He began shouting loudly at her. "You're nothing but a two-dollar cunt. That's spelled c.u.n.t. You know what that means, don't you? You've been laying down for two dollars all your life."

Sinatra stuffed two one-dollar bills in the empty cocktail glass she held in her hand, continuing his tirade:

"Here's two dollars, baby. That's what you're used to. You scum, go home and take a bath. Print that, Mrs. Cheshire. I'm getting out of here to rid myself of the stench of Mrs. Cheshire."

Mrs. Cheshire burst into tears. While the Republican Party hierarchs watched appalled, Sinatra stormed out of the hotel. When the reporter recovered, she hired Edward Bennett Williams to file a million-dollar suit against Sinatra. "If Sinatra had attacked me as a reporter, I would have taken it. But he attacked me as a woman," she said. The mother of four children, she went on: "I feel I owe it to my children to sue. I'm square enough that virtue means something to me."

When news of this fracas reached the Oval Office, it was reported that the president was "furious." It was not an unexpected reaction from a man who abhorred public crudity and bridled at the tiniest personal slight to any woman.

After a long silence, Victor Gold, Agnew's press secretary, offered the vice-president's statement: "Maxine Cheshire has a carapace of an armadillo."

The lawsuit never materialized. Was there an under-the-table payoff? To this day no one except those on the inside can know for sure.

In spite of Sinatra's scene with Maxine Cheshire in Washington, *and* his appearance before the House committee, President Nixon invited him to perform at the White House on April 17, 1973. Perhaps the reason was Sinatra's contribution of $50,000 to the reelection campaign of the president, whom he publicly supported. The White House appearance was technically in honor of the visiting prime minister of Italy, Giulio Andreotti.

He sang "The House I Live In," and the president beamed with satisfaction while Pat Nixon kept time by nodding her head.

The president spoke about the entertainer in this fashion: "Once in a while, there is a moment when there is magic in the room, when a singer is able to move us and capture us all, and Frank Sinatra has done that and we thank him."

At the end of the program, for perhaps the first time in his public life, Sinatra was in tears.

★ 12 ★

Reprise

Even as he stood there in the White House listening to the words of President Nixon, his eyes filling with tears, Frank Sinatra was remembering Nixon's words when he introduced him earlier that evening. The president called the singer "the Washington Monument of Entertainment." And he said, "This house is honored to have a man whose parents were born in Italy and who from humble beginnings rose to the very top of the entertainment world." Moreover, at the end of the concert, it was the president himself who approached Sinatra and said in a low voice, "You must get out of retirement."

And Sinatra replied, "Mr. President, after tonight, I'll have to think about it."

Within days of his appearance at the White House, Sinatra made his decision. A newspaper story reported that he was planning an NBC-TV special, penciled in for November 11, 1973. Then, about the middle of June, a front-page story in the *Los Angeles Times* said that he was going to "unretire." He said he would appear in public only when he could "control the situation." "I'm not going to put myself in the position of facing big, uncontrolled crowds again. Too many times, I became the victim in such situations, and I'm not going to let that happen again." He would make records, sing before small groups of friends, and do television specials. "That can be controlled."

And, on September 20, 1973, he was taping the NBC show and was talking about his so-called retirement. He admitted, "I didn't find retirement all that I expected it to be. I was under constant pressure to return to work."

Perhaps. Most of that pressure was probably exerted by himself.

The "one-more-time" show was broadcast on November 18. One columnist, Joyce Haber, previewed it and came up with this comment: "The show that you'll see on November 18 is called *Magnavox Presents Frank Sinatra*. It might have been called The Reincarnation of the King."

The special was a hit. After his first song, Sinatra talked about his "retirement" and "return."

"I didn't know how much I'd miss the business—the records, the movies, the saloons. So here I am for all the young people who wanted to know what I *used* to work like."

In January 1974, Sinatra opened at Caesars Palace in Las Vegas, where he wowed them once again. He was back in harness for good—and the public rejoiced.

The public—but not necessarily the press. Even in his "retirement," Sinatra had been thinking about his relationship with the members of the media. He had once hinted that he had left show business in order to avoid the constant pressure of having the press peering in at him.

In a *TV Guide* article, he said to Dwight Whitney: "In retirement it was worse than ever. Some of the picayune stuff would cease but there was always the press. I call them garbage collectors, the columnists without a conscience, the reporters who take long shots based on the idea that where there's smoke, there's fire. I'm blunt and I'm honest. I could call them pimps and whores."

Yeah. And in July 1974, it was quite suddenly—and resoundingly—obvious that the feud was still on. The occasion was an extensive singing tour of Australia, dreamed up to duplicate a very satisfactory circuit he had made Down Under in 1959. This time Sinatra took Barbara Marx with him, Jilly Rizzo, and his lawyer, Milton "Mickey" Rudin. His publicist, Jim Mahoney, stayed home. This was going to be a new Sinatra, fresh from retirement, and happy in his work. Hell, he had had a very good warm-up at Las Vegas in January, and a reprise in March had shown that he was as limber as ever. It was time to unveil the new Sinatra.

But in spite of all the good intentions and the promises, promises, promises . . .

In Melbourne, Sinatra was en route to a rehearsal when a woman television reporter stopped him and asked him for an interview. Of course, without Mahoney present there was no one who could tell her that Sinatra never gave interviews off the cuff. How it started no one remembered, but soon there was a fight among guards, reporters, and photographers. Photographers were pushed out of the way, and someone tied the cord of a television camera around a cameraman's neck.

After the rehearsal, Sinatra was besieged by the media, and lashed out at them in his familiar way: "Bums, parasites, hookers, and pimps," was the colorful way he put it. He wanted to talk mostly about women reporters. "They are the hookers of the press," he told them. "Need I explain to you? I might offer them a buck and a half." Then he remembered Maxine Cheshire. "I once paid a broad in Washington two dollars. I overpaid her, I found out. She didn't even bathe. Most of them don't."

Australia wasn't America, Frank soon found out. The head of the Labor party in New South Wales was mightily exercised by Sinatra's attack. "Who the hell does this man Sinatra think he is?" demanded Melville Wren. The Transport Workers Union said it would boycott Sinatra and refused to service his private jet. If it made good on this threat, the $650,000 tour would be scuttled before it started. Sinatra was not just angry now; he was frantic about the financial disaster that faced him.

Labor leader Bob Hawke flew in from Melbourne to Sydney to meet in Sinatra's hotel suite. Prolonged negotiations ensued between Hawke and Rudin. "If you do not express regrets," Hawke told Sinatra through Rudin, exhibiting a bit of Aussie humor, "your stay in Australia might be indefinite, unless you can walk across water." Statements from both sides eventually appeared, statements so blurred with equivocation as to be meangingless.

The journalists admitted that their "pursuit of Sinatra over five days had been a little provocative." Sinatra apologized for injuries "as a result of attempts to ensure his personal safety," but he reserved the right in the future to attack journalists "subject to criticism on professional grounds." In addition, Sinatra promised to do a big free television show that the whole country could see. One newspaper wrote: "Without Henry Kissinger's intervention, peace had been made."

There were the usual pictures. One showed Frank Sinatra in dark glasses. Another showed Barbara Marx in dark glasses.

During his concert in Melbourne, Sinatra sat on a stool and began talking off the cuff to the audience. "We've been having a marvelous time being chased around the country," he said. "We came all this way to Australia because I chose to come back here and because I haven't been here in a long time and I wanted to come back." But then: "So we come here and what happens? Gotta run all day long because of the parasites who chased us, with automobiles. It's dangerous, it could cause an accident, they won't quit, they wonder why I won't talk to them. I won't drink their water, let alone not talk to them."

And about the media generally, "I say they're bums and they're always going to be bums. There are a few exceptions to the rule, some good editorial writers who don't go out in the street and chase people around." As for the Australian press in particular: "What I see has happened since I was here, sixteen years ago, the type of news they print in this town has shocked me. It's old-fashioned. It was done in America and England twenty years ago, and they're catching up now with the scandal sheets. You use them to train your dog and your parrot. It's the best thing to do with it—or set fire to one of their cars."

In the *Morning Herald* Sydney journalist Lenore Nicklin wrote: "Seventy of us parasites, bums, and unwashed hookers brushed up as best we could for a press conference given by Mr. Frank Sinatra's lawyer, Mr. Milton A. Rudin. [Rudin] said he didn't want to lecture the press, then proceeded to do so. [Danny O'Donovan, one of the tour promoters] contributed a number of sentences which mostly began with 'At this point in time.'" One of Sinatra's last gestures was to pose with Prime Minister Gough Whitlam for a photo. But Sinatra insisted that a professional photographer be hired, rather than allowing the press a photo opportunity. The papers refused to print the picture.

At about this time Don Rickles appeared with Bob Hope on a television show. Rickles said, "Frank just called me—he's declared war on Australia." Hope responded, "You know why those Aussie labor leaders gave in? I think one of them found a kangaroo head on his pillow." (This was an obvious reference to the famous scene in *The Godfather,* allegedly based on Sinatra's career.)

Later on, Hope remarked: "Frank spoke about 'buck-and-a-half hookers.' What a memory *he* has!"

Back in the States, it wasn't long before Sinatra found himself involved in a weird court case involving a skirmish in the men's room of a Palm Springs hotel. The whole thing started when Sinatra apparently took umbrage at the attitude of a young businessman named Frank Weinstock. The silly battle was over the question of who was ogling whose woman! It was Jilly Rizzo who allegedly took matters into his own hands and administered a "beating" to the man in question. The altercation resulted in a heavy fine for assault and battery, lodged against Rizzo. But after a new notices in the press, the affair blew over.

Sinatra was back. And he was beginning to wow

them all over again. Madison Square Garden in October 1974 was the scene of what was billed as *The Main Event*. The boxing motif was carried out in the stage design. Sinatra sang on a raised platform that looked exactly like a boxing ring, with the audience of 21,000 seated around him on all sides. The whole show was also to be shown on television, beamed to all corners of the world equipped with television sets, on the following Sunday night.

As Sinatra entered the "ring," he was introduced by gravel-voiced, Bronx-accented Howard Cosell— long a favorite of Sinatra's—in Cosell's typical rasping, aggressive, macho, and witty manner. Sinatra appeared in what his daughter Nancy later called his "Dracula outfit"—white scarf, black overcoat, with wing-type collars—and from the beginning he had them in the palms of his hands.

But not all the critics agreed. Take Dermot Purgavie of the London *Daily Mail*: "The contemptuous crudity of his recent public behavior has made even some of his most passionate admirers concede that ego, money, power or whatever gratification stimulated his return to performing overshadowed good judgment and instead of calling women journalists 'whores'—and worse—he should finally call it quits."

George Frazier, in the *Boston Globe,* wrote: "The trouble with you, Frankie, is you got no style. All your life you wanted to be a big man but the wrong kind of big man. Look, Sinatra, Momo Giancana is just another version of Haldeman, and Agnew makes three. You're a sad case, Frankie. I think you're the best male vocalist who ever lived, but I also think you're a miserable failure as a human being."

But the *New York Times* loved him. Its Sunday Arts and Leisure section had an eight-column banner titled "That Old Sinatra Magic Is a Mix of Musicianship and Sex Appeal," with two long articles praising him. John Rockwell found the show "superb," the audience "rapturous," and Sinatra "the master of his generation."

Nevertheless, the show was not a ratings triumph. It failed by three points to achieve the 30 percent share that was regarded as a water mark of a show's success. The general consensus was that Sinatra had flopped in the ratings. To make matters worse for 1974 generally, the Lady Journalists of Hollywood voted him "Sour Apple of the Year."

In 1975 he went to Canada and Europe—and had a few bad days. In Toronto a photographer claimed that one of Sinatra's bodyguards had punched him. Sinatra offered a million dollars to the photographer if he could prove it. There was no answer—but plenty of press.

In Germany he was on the receiving end again. Empty seats dotted concert halls where he was appearing. He even got a kidnap threat in Berlin and canceled his show. The press implied that he had done so in order to avoid singing to an empty hall. He was even termed a "super gangster" and a "pathetic alcoholic," although the terms suffer in translation.

But in London in May they loved him. He told 7,000 cheering people in the audience: "I could have answered them [the German press] and told reporters to look to the sins of their fathers. I could have mentioned Dachau. *They* are the gangsters." And back in the States, Sinatra appeared with John

Denver at Harrah's on Lake Tahoe—in what was billed as "the entertainment coup of the decade." Records show that there were 672,412 requests for seats at that show.

He also had two hugely successful weeks at the Uris Theater in New York, where he starred with Count Basie and Ella Fitzgerald. Those shows grossed over $1 million. Even the press admitted that Frank Sinatra was probably the biggest attraction to play Broadway in modern times. He raised an enormous amount of money later in the year when he appeared on the Jerry Lewis Labor Day Telethon for Muscular Distrophy. That ended 1975 on a high note—a good omen for 1976, which indeed proved to be a very good year.

On July 11, 1976, Frank Sinatra married Barbara Blakely Marx at the two-hundred-acre Palm Springs estate of Walter Annenberg, a former ambassador to Great Britain and the publisher of *TV Guide*. Freeman Gosden, of the old *Amos 'n' Andy* show was best man, and Beatrice Korshak, a Los Angeles attorney, was matron of honor. Present were the Ronald Reagans, the Gregory Pecks, and the Kirk Douglases. As the priest asked the bride, "Do you take this man for richer, for poorer . . ." Frank Sinatra was heard to murmur in an audible stage whisper: "Richer, richer!"

A reception including about 125 people followed at Sinatra's Rancho Mirage compound. He gave his bride a peacock-blue Rolls-Royce. Barbara gave him a gray Jaguar.

Sinatra basked contentedly in the adulation of his friends. "I really have found some kind of wonderful tranquillity," he said. "What the hell, it's about time. I'm at a very happy part in life. Barbara is a marvelous woman, a great gal."

In April 1978 Sinatra flew to Israel to dedicate the Frank Sinatra International Student Center, located at the Mount Scopus campus of the Hebrew University, in Jerusalem. The center was to house facilities for thousands of students from America, Australia, Canada, Africa, and Europe. It stands near the Harry S. Truman Research Institute of Archaeology, the Martin Buber Center for Adult Study, and the Albert Einstein Institute. "I had a street education, from the gutter to the curbstone," Sinatra told those assembled at the dedication. "I am self-taught, but have learned a lot from listening to people with great knowledge. Education is what it is all about. I hope it will eventually wipe out the lack of tolerance, and that brotherhood and peace may spread throughout the world."

The next year he was singing in the shadow of the Sphinx and the Pyramids in behalf of Cairo's Faith and Rehabilitation Center, a charity of the wife of former Egyptian president Gramal Abdel Nasser. It was a unique concert, part of a three-day gala that would raise a half-million dollars. "It's the biggest room I've ever played, and the toughest act I've ever followed," he told the guests who were seated before him on Persian carpets.

Two months later Caesars Palace in Las Vegas was throwing a huge party to celebrate Sinatra's fortieth year in show business. It was a massive sellout.

In October 1979 Sinatra starred in *Sinatra at the Met* held at the Metropolitan Opera House in Lincoln Center, where he helped raise $1,100,000 for the Memorial Sloan-Kettering Cancer Center.

By September 1980 he was back in London for a series of concerts at both the Royal Festival and the Royal Albert Halls. There Derek Jewell, the critic of *The Sunday Times* wrote: "Sinatra has become the keeper of the flame for everyone from forty to eighty. His songs distill the youth, the nostalgia of millions. He also happens to be the best at it: an artist of colossal stature. He swings, he speaks, he shapes songs like no one else. That's genius."

Sinatra had not only unretired from singing but from motion pictures. In October 1980 he returned to make *The First Deadly Sin* with Faye Dunaway. Based on the best-selling novel by Lawrence Sanders, about a retired New York cop after a serial killer, the picture did well in the States and abroad.

The year 1980 was, of course, an election year. Sinatra, with his friend Dean Martin, had begun their political activities as early as November 1979, when the two of them helped launch Ronald Reagan's bid for the presidential nomination. They had chosen Boston for the kickoff. "I am thrilled, overjoyed, humbled, and, most of all, honored that I have been chosen for the job twice in my lifetime," Sinatra said. "And I am especially happy that I will have done it for our *two* great political parties."

And so in 1981 it was no particular surprise when Ronald Reagan, the new president, selected Sinatra to produce his inauguration gala.

It was a doozie. Johnny Carson was emcee, Bob Hope and Rich Little were star comics, and the cast of superstars included Ben Vereen, Ethel Merman, Charlton Heston, Debby Boone, Donny and Marie Osmond.

There was even a Sammy Cahn parody of "Nancy

(with the Laughing Face)" rewritten to fit Nancy Reagan. "I'm so proud that you're First Lady, Nancy," the new words went, "and I'm so pleased that I'm sort of a chum. The next eight years will be fancy, as fancy as they come."

At the climax of the show, Jimmy Stewart wheeled out onto the stage General Omar Bradley, eighty-seven, the five-star hero of World War II. It was a three-hour gala—and proof that Sinatra could still hack it with the best.

Rumors of Sinatra's gangland connections would keep surfacing again and again—and 1981 was no exception. But this time the situation was a bit different. The singer now decided he wanted to get back the Nevada gaming license he had lost in 1963. He needed the license to become a public-relations consultant for Caesars Palace. And he proved that he had, at long last, learned how to present his difficult associations with mobsters in a more or less appealing vein.

One question put to him was: "Mr. Sinatra, were you ever acquainted with Matthew Ianella?"

"I don't think so," mused Sinatra. "What's his alias?"

"Mattie the Horse."

"Oh, yeah," said Sinatra, his face lighting up.

"Willie Moretti?"

"Mr. Moretti," Sinatra said in his pulpit voice, "had absolutely nothing to do with my career."

"Did you ever fly to Havana with two million dollars in an attaché case?"

"Show me an attaché case that can hold two million dollars and you can have the two million."

"Why did you go to Havana?"

"To find sunshine."

"When you were about to lose your gaming license in 1963, did you call up Ed Olsen, the head of the control board, and threaten him?"

"I wonder if there's a human alive that hasn't lost his temper," Sinatra mused. "We've taken a four-minute conversation and made it into an international incident."

He explained away a photograph showing him in the company of New York godfather Carlo Gambino and a number of other companions as the work of mobster Aladena Fratianno, who had written about Sinatra in his "memoirs" and wanted to be shown with him. Sinatra said that he was posing for a picture with a child backstage at the Westchester Premier Theater in Tarrytown, New York. "Before I knew what had happened, there were eight or nine men standing around me." Posing backstage was all part of his job, Sinatra explained. "When I'm asked to pose [with] three Chinamen in Hong Kong . . . I don't ask for a sputum test."

P.S.: He got the license. His success impressed not a few people—including those who might be able to make use of the singer's new sophisticated persona.

In 1981, the Golden Nugget opened in Atlantic City—a resort area that was trying to out-Vegas Las Vegas. Steve Wynn had obtained a permanent license to operate the place, and from the moment it opened, the facility was a big moneymaker, earning $17,700,000 in the first six months of operation. It was so phenomenally successful, in fact, that Wynn hired Frank Sinatra for $10 million plus, guaranteed over three years, to become the "label" of the Golden Nugget, to appear in its television commercials, and to gamble at the casino to attract customers. For perks, Sinatra would get the use of Wynn's $13 million Boeing 727, his helicopters, and his limousines, and be able to stay in one of the lavish suites for high-rollers built at a cost of $4,500,000. "What I wanted Sinatra to help us do rather than just pack the house—which he could do on a desert island anywhere—was to help us build the bond of affection between our employees and our customers," Wynn said.

Sinatra was a big draw at the Golden Nugget. It was said that during his first appearance, the casino brought in $20 million in receipts. There were a number of true high-rollers in the audience. One man, it was reported, lost $3,700,000 at the baccarat tables. Although this was not a person in any way associated with or related to Frank Sinatra, it was obvious that the appeal of the Sinatra image did bring in what the casino owners would call the "right people"—the swingers, the big spenders, the true gamblers.

Yet it seemed that all Frank Sinatra had learned about handling his associations with mobsters, and about handling *himself* in an emergency, evaporated in a showdown. Such a confrontation occurred in Atlantic City toward the end of 1983.

On December 1, when Sinatra was performing at the Golden Nugget Casino, he, his wife Barbara, and his buddy Dean Martin began gambling at the blackjack table. Everything went along smoothly until Sinatra suddenly became impatient with the dealer, a Chinese-American woman named Kyong Kim. She seemed to be having trouble dealing the cards from the dealing shoe. Sinatra suggested that she hold a single deck in her hand and deal from it.

"He was very mad at me," she said later, "for being so slow." Although she was frightened, she quite calmly explained to him that he was asking her to do something that was against the law. The New Jersey Casino Control Commission insisted that all blackjack cards be dealt out of a shoe holding six decks of cards.

This didn't satisfy Sinatra. "You don't want to play one deck," he yelled, "you go back to China!" Suddenly the Mr. Hyde side of the famed Sinatra multipersonality was in the ascendant.

Kim stood her ground. The pit boss, Maxwell Spinks, now got into the act. He said later that Sinatra was "loud" and "abusive" to Kim. The entertainer seemed to be "pumping himself up into a very dictatorial attitude." But Spinks did not feel he could stop the game because he was afraid that "all hell would break loose." He had heard about Sinatra, and he felt that the singer would "hit the roof."

The brouhaha now attracted the attention of the next up in the command hierarchy—the floor manager, a woman named Joyce Caparale. One of her jobs was to supervise the blackjack table. She too knew about Sinatra's background, his Jekyll-Hyde personality, and his penchant for getting employees fired in Vegas when he didn't like them. She said she was afraid to "ruffle [his] feathers," and approached the fray apprehensively. While she was trying to restore order, Sinatra yelled at Maxwell Spinks, the pit boss, and "got really irritated"—in Caparale's words.

"I want a single deck, and if I don't get it, I won't be putting on my show!" It was obvious Sinatra was in one of his really offensive rages. His wife and

Dean Martin were trying to quiet him, but it did no good. He started to holler loudly. When the pit boss finally came over, Sinatra waved him off as if he was some kind of messenger boy.

"I'm not going to perform if you don't deal out of a single deck!" he shouted at Kim.

"He scared the heck out of me," Caparale said later.

Now the shift manager, Robert Barnum, approached. He too knew about Sinatra's eccentricities and feared them. He thought of the entertainer as someone special who had to be placated "at any risk." With Sinatra's threat not to perform at the Golden Nugget still hanging in the air, Barnum gave the signal.

And so at that point the dealer, the pit boss, the floor manager, *and* the shift manager all caved in. Kim dealt to Sinatra out of a deck of hand-held cards.

It did not take long for this infraction of the rules to come to the attention of the New Jersey Casino Control Commission. All four employees whom Sinatra had cowed were suspended for various periods of time. The Golden Nugget itself was fined $25,000. Sinatra and Martin were called in and both apologized for the fracas and the misunderstanding. They pleaded innocent because they were "unaware" of the rules of the New Jersey commission. In fact, Sinatra and Martin offered to pay the salaries of the four suspended employees.

Even Nugget owner Steve Wynn got into the act. He told the commission that Sinatra and Martin did not have to pay the salaries, that the employees would remain suspended. He said that the two Hollywood stars were "just out to have a little fun.

Sinatra and Martin were both unaware of the fact that the law was broken. They told me that if they had known it was against the law, they wouldn't have done it."

The commissioner, Joel Jacobson, chastised the Golden Nugget management for being too easy on the entertainers and for not getting sworn statements from them as they had from the employees. Jacobson called Sinatra an "obnoxious bully" and categorized him as a man who "forced working men and women to commit infractions because of the fear of losing their jobs." He said that some celebrities like Sinatra occasionally had an "unfortunate combination of an uncluttered mind and a bloated ego."

Sinatra would not let that remark remain unanswered. He stewed about it for a while, then suddenly made an announcement in the press that he had canceled all future engagements at the Golden Nugget Casino in Atlantic City. In fact, he went on to say, he had canceled the state of New Jersey as well, had crossed it off his list for good. And he had been born there! Mickey Rudin said that his client would not sing in a state whose officials used him as a "punching bag."

However, his $10 million contract would remain in force, and his fourteen appearance dates at the Atlantic City Golden Nugget would be shifted to Caesars Palace in Las Vegas—owned by the same group who owned the Nugget.

Wynn was angry with the sensation-hungry media, which had "turned a minor incident into international headlines." The publicity that ensued created nothing but, in his words, "pain, humiliation, and embarrassment" for the management.

As Wynn saw it, the members of his staff had overreacted to Sinatra's presence. The singer, he said, was "a forceful, assertive man trying to get what he wanted, believing strongly that he was well within the law in taking that position."

In time it all simmered down, and quite soon Sinatra was appearing once again at the Golden Nugget in Atlantic City, along with his other engagements all over the world.

Mixed in with the good and the bad, one piece of information loomed most imposingly on the horizon. Sinatra's spies had discovered that Kitty Kelley, a newspaper writer who had produced two successful biographies of celebrities, was preparing an unauthorized biography of Frank Sinatra.

When Kelley realized that Sinatra was aware of her project, she immediately announced that she was indeed going to write just such a book. "Most journalists who even ask the mean, excitable Sinatra what he thinks of the weather are likely to find themselves in the Potomac River," Kelley told a reporter for the *London Daily Mirror*. When the reporter asked her how much she was going to be paid for her book, Kelley said: "A million dollars plus a choice of funeral gown to be laid out in."

Now Sinatra went to work. He got his staff to churn out hundreds of letters, and sent them to every one of his contacts—friends *and* enemies—warning them that to help Kelley in her research would be a mistake. To put it mildly. In addition, he announced that he would be writing his *own* autobiography to offset Kelley's unofficial—and thus, he intimated, not fully authentic—work. He also went to court, claiming that Kelley had misrepresented herself in claiming that she had his permission to ask questions. He also claimed that he and he alone had the right to exploit his name and image. *That* was the crux of the case.

Now a group called Reporters for Freedom of the Press rallied and contended that Sinatra's attempt to thwart Kelley in her writing was a serious affront to *anyone* trying to write a book about a famous person. And Sinatra's contention that only he had the right to exploit his name and image angered the National Writers' Union and the American Society of Journalists and Authors. They defended Kelley's right to go on with her work. Michael Wheland, president of the Washington Independent Writers' Society said, "This is a chilling example of how a powerful public figure, using money and influence, can orchestrate what the public shall know about him."

During this exchange, Kelley went into seclusion, surfacing occasionally—once to point out gleefully that all the publicity had flushed out a number of people who had offered to give her information because they didn't like Sinatra's attitude.

Kelley's book appeared in 1986 and became an immediate and overwhelming best-seller. Its success overshadowed by far a beautifully produced, extensively researched, extremely competent book by Nancy Sinatra titled *Frank Sinatra: My Father,* which had been published in hardcover in 1985 and was released in paperback in 1986.

In 1983, Frank Sinatra had received the Kennedy Center Award for Lifetime Achievement, with both the president and Mrs. Ronald Reagan present to pay homage to him and the four other honorees for his lifelong achievements in the performing arts.

In the September years of his life, and in the reprise of those September years, Sinatra had indeed become a legend—perhaps even a myth. And that myth was somewhat tarnished and seemed in need of polishing. Could it be that the image was just slightly out of focus? Could a closer look at the man and the myth—as seen and known by his numerous friends, enemies, and associates—clear up the mystery?

★ 13 ★

A Profile of Contrasts

In early November 1986 Frank Sinatra was playing an engagement at the Golden Nugget in Atlantic City. He had been performing fairly regularly that year, but with a few interruptions during the preceding two months. An operation for intestinal polyps early in 1986 forced him to cancel several performances in the late summer. Now, as he opened on Thursday night, he began to experience extreme pain, and on Friday night it was one of those "the show must go on" things. By Saturday, he decided that he would be unable to perform. Instead, he boarded his private jet Saturday afternoon and flew to Palm Springs; there he was rushed to Rancho Mirage and the Eisenhower Medical Center for an immediate operation to remove an abscess from his large intestine.

He was suffering, according to his personal physician, Dr. Alan Altman, from acute diverticulitis. After a two-hour operation, during which a twelve-inch section of his intestine was removed, he was hospitalized for seven to ten days. "He's experiencing a lot of pain, and despite medication and antibiotics, he continues to experience pain," his physician reported. There was absolutely no evidence of complication or cancer, a hospital spokesperson reported.

A simple enough operation, an almost routine surgical performance. Yet when it happened to Frank Sinatra, it became headline stuff. Both New York tabloids carried streamers about the incident in their first editions on the following Monday. The news editors knew that Sinatra had been operated on earlier in the year in May—once for two polyps removed from his colon, and once for the removal of a basal cell carcinoma, a form of skin cancer, from under his right eye.

These two danger signals must have been in their minds as they studied the report of Sinatra's flight to Rancho Mirage and the medical readout that followed.

It would be natural for most newspapermen in such a situation to think briefly about clearing the decks for action—just in case. Perhaps most of them did indeed sneak a look at Sinatra's packet in the obit files to check it out for proper updating. And in doing so, most of them must have wondered how the story should be handled, if . . .

What, in fact, was the status of Frank Sinatra's image in winter 1986? How would they play him? What would determine the final public outlook on the man and the myth that was Frank Sinatra?

The basic problem, of course, was his personality; from the beginning this man had been an unbelievable composite of opposites. For every person who loved him, there was probably at least one who hated and loathed him. He could charm the birds down out of the trees at one moment, and in the next turn the entire population against him. Many of his close acquaintances had actually talked of him in terms of the Dr. Jekyll and Mr. Hyde syndrome.

He could be vibrant, vital, loving—a real role model for anyone. But he was a mixture of conflicting moods. He could be the epitome of politeness—and he could be the rudest man in the world. He could be assured—and he could be insecure. He could be warm and tender—and he could be tough and arrogant. His charisma always drew the public eye toward him; and then as his fans watched, he exposed every nerve fiber of his being.

He ran, in the trite phrase, the gamut of all human emotions. He could be sensitive and vulnerable, or he would be rock-hard and ice-cold. Comic or amusing, or tragic and foreboding. Tolerant, or intolerant. Sociable and friendly, or aloof and haughty. Modest and unassuming one moment, or brash and overbearing the next. He was the most generous man in the world, if you happened to be on the receiving end of one of his charitable contributions. But he could be tight-fisted and a terror in business, who would push you to the wall and laugh as you were stripped bare.

But whether he was good or bad, decent or indecent, nice guy or boor, it must be remembered about Sinatra that everything he ever accomplished—on both sides of the weighing scale—was done from one specific source of power and authority.

And that center was *music* and Sinatra's ability to *sing.*

He used this ability from the very beginning. At first he sang to his peers—particularly the girls—but of course it wasn't long before his audience expanded to people of all ages. It was disk jockey William B. Williams, of WNEW, a lifelong admirer of Sinatra and the man who nicknamed him the "chairman of the board," who summed up the essence of Sinatra: "You get the feeling that he is living life to the hilt, getting all there is to get from every moment. In 'Come Fly with Me' you say, 'Boy, here's a guy who's got it made and he knows, as we know, that it's all transitory so he's going to grab it while he can.'"

Indeed, living life to the hilt was a Sinatra essential—as exemplified by the titles of many of his best songs: "All or Nothing at All," "All of Me," "All the Way," "My Way." It is life he has always celebrated. "You got to love living, baby. Dying's a pain in the ass," he once remarked from the stage at Harrah's, for no particular reason. But it seemed to be his outlook on life.

One student of Sinatra—Mitchell Fink—put it this way: "Sinatra is a mirror image of the songs he made famous. His personality—whether you think he's a lovable rogue, or a merry prankster, or a man who hits photographers, or even a Godfather—is merely a by-product of his life in music. The music in Frank Sinatra's life will always come first."

It is in his music that he endures and will endure. To get a view of this complex man is not an easy thing. Thomas Thompson, a former editor of *Life* magazine and a man who knew and respected him, once wrote an article in *McCall's* called "Understanding Sinatra," in which he said: "I cannot begin to understand this man—indeed, I doubt if he understands himself."

And he went on to say: "One key to Frank is that he relishes power. He revels in it more than any public figure I can think of. . . . Perhaps his reasoning is that because he has occupied for so long a time the summit position in show business, this entitles him to sit as an equal at the table of other kings—those of industry, medicine, politics, government."

James Bacon, a journalist who has been quoted many times regarding Sinatra, once wrote: "His moods are as varied as his songs. When he's charming, Cary Grant could take lessons from him. When he isn't, Muhammad Ali should. . . . Probably the main reason that Frank has people like Jilly [Rizzo] and comedian Pat Henry around him much of the time is because Frank doesn't like to be alone. . . . Frank is probably the most complex man in show business. And that, of course, is what makes him Frank."

But why the animosity toward the press? Why the constant badgering of reporters and photographers, who, for God's sake, are only trying to do their job?

"I think that he's always nurtured a secret desire to be a hood," Bing Crosby once said. "But, of course, he's got too much class, too much sense, to go that route—so he gets his kicks out of barking at newsmen and so forth."

Gay Talese tried to point up the complexities and the strange inconsistencies in the Sinatra character some years ago. He explained how Sinatra always tried to do certain things in a very *personal* manner. At Christmas, for example, he would *personally* pick out dozens of presents for his close friends and family, remembering the type of jewelry they liked, their favorite colors, even the sizes of their shirts and dresses.

And he was able to be marvelously helpful and do unforgettable things for people in trouble. When a musician's house was destroyed and his wife killed in a Los Angeles mud slide, Sinatra was there almost immediately. He personally came to the man's aid, finding him a new home, paying whatever hospital bills were left unpaid by the insurance, and then personally supervising the furnishing of a new home for him, down to the replacing of the silverware and the linen and the purchase of new clothing.

But as we've seen, there was also the Mr. Hyde side of Sinatra. One of his assistants once brought him a frankfurter with ketchup on it; as it happened, the poor man didn't realize that Sinatra hated ketchup. The singer threw the whole bottle at the man, splattering it all over him.

And then, on another occasion, he might act the role of the perfect gentleman. A friend of his daughter Nancy once came to a party at the house. Early on, she accidentally knocked over one of a pair of beautiful alabaster birds. The statuette fell to the floor, shattering into a million pieces. Nancy Jr. turned pale. "Oh," she gasped, "that was one of mother's favorite—"

Sinatra cut her off with a glare. As forty guests in the room all gaped in apprehensive silence, Sinatra moved quickly over to the table and pushed the other bird off, smashing it to bits on the floor beside the first.

He then put his arm around his daughter's friend, and said, in a way that made it all right forever, "That's okay, kid."

But then, in the next moment—who knows?

"My feeling about Frank," Burt Lancaster said, "is that he is basically a lonely person. . . . Maybe that is why Frank is always having a big bunch of hangers-on about him. He's a marvelous host." And he was "liberal," too, Lancaster felt. (He was speaking in 1972.) "He always has had strong feelings about the rights of people, coming as he does from a background in which Italian people were legislated against in the early days much as blacks and Chicanos are today."

Lancaster went on: "Frank is very, very independent of spirit. . . . He is a man of fierce loyalties. . . . He is a very paternalistic man and worries about his daughters. . . . He is a very stern father—fair-minded but stern."

As for happiness? "Is Frank a happy man? I don't know. I don't know if it is possible for him to be happy in the sense that we think of happiness. Frank is too sensitive a man, too involved in problems that are personal, and also problems that are related to the conditions of the world, not to be distressed by them."

Sammy Davis, Jr., was always one of Sinatra's most ardent admirers. At benefits and wherever he performed, he was usually very open on the subject of Frank Sinatra. "I do not genuflect when he walks into the room," he might say. "Do I owe him a lot for the help he's given me? You bet your bird I do. He knocked on a lot of doors I couldn't get into. I would not be standing on this stage today if I hadn't had his help." He once remarked, "People say I idolize Frank. All right. I got a picture taken at the Capital Theater of Frank and my mother. He said to my mother, 'I hope you know your son is going to be one of our biggest stars.' Years later he walked over to my mother and said, 'See, I told you!' That makes up for all the other bullshit. When you need him, he's there."

And then one night Sammy Davis, Jr., was trying

to explain his good friend and mentor to a television audience—explain him honestly, with all the warts as well as the beauty spots. It went this way: "I love Frank, but there are many things he does that there is no excuse for. I don't care if you are the most talented person in the world. It does not give you the right to step on people and treat them rotten. This is what he does occasionally."

Good-bye, Sam! What he had said was no more than a self-evident truth, but when Frank Sinatra heard about it, he turned a cold shoulder on this very close friend—and that cold shoulder lasted for many months. A thaw did eventually set in, but the relationship was never the same as it had been before.

Davis was not alone in that chilly limbo Sinatra managed to create about him as a special type of punishment. The connection between Sinatra and Peter Lawford had already been severed by the fancied defection of Lawford during the Kennedy–Sinatra disconnection. The story goes that Davis and Lawford met each other on the Sunset Strip one day and were comparing notes on their status with Frank Sinatra. The consensus was that Davis was definitely out, but that Lawford had a good chance of being reinstated. "He still has my picture on the piano," Lawford said.

It was actress Rosalind Russell, a person quite close to Sinatra for years, who summed him up in this way: "Frank Sinatra is an American classic. . . . To be Frank's friend is like one of his songs: 'All or Nothing at All.' It is a total, unconditional commitment, a never-fraying security blanket." As for a one-word label, she said: "To describe Sinatra in one word I respond without hesitation: *compas-*

sionate. I have never seen him refuse a child any-thing."

But there was that Jekyll-Hyde duality. "There are several Sinatras," she explained. "Perhaps this is what makes him both fascinating and controver-sial. He is tempestuous, tender, searching, indefati-gable, unexpected. As a father, he is doting, generous, always involved. . . . The perfect host, there is [also] Sinatra the loner, the constant observer, a profoundly sensitive man."

And yet—and yet . . .

In his autobiography, Eddie Fisher described Sinatra:

"Frank wore his emotions on his sleeve and I always thought his cocky, tough-guy attitude was probably just a way of protecting himself from being hurt. He seemed to prefer respect to love and when he thought he had been insulted he was like a wild man. I saw his quick temper flare while we were together in London."

That happened in 1963, after Sinatra had just finished a worldwide tour. Fisher visited him in his suite at Claridge's. Kidding Sinatra, Fisher greeted him with these words: "Good morning, Your High-ness."

It turned out that one of the guests—a young woman with a scarf around her head—was Princess Alexandra, a *real* highness. The laugh was on Fisher. He then enjoyed a relaxed chat with Sinatra, the princess, and other guests.

Somehow word of the princess's visit got out to the press, and a big story appeared. Sinatra blew his top. He vowed at the top of his voice to "get" the guy who had told the reporters. One by one he buttonholed all his friends, demanding to know which one had told the reporters about the princess's visit.

The night before Sinatra was leaving for the States, he had another party, at which he was still glowering at everybody. "I've narrowed it down to two people!" he announced as he circulated the suite. "The assistant manager of the hotel and the elevator operator. I want everybody here tomorrow morning at ten!" It was apparently going to be an Agatha Christie session in which Sinatra would point the finger of accusation and exact punishment.

Fisher tried to reason with him. "Frank, these things happen," he told him. "Forget it. You've just come off this marvelous world tour. Don't blow it now." Fisher wrote: "*I* was worried about Sinatra's image."

Sinatra didn't see it that way. Quickly he turned on Fisher and his eyes blazed. "Who the fuck asked you?"

Another of Sinatra's longtime companions, Dean Martin, once said that to get along with Sinatra, you simply didn't talk about anything *deep*. You just kidded around and never got to the bottom of anything. "I don't discuss his girl with Frank or who he's going to marry. All I discuss are movies, TV, golf, and drinking."

Martin had a relaxed way about him that intrigued audiences and sometimes fooled people who didn't see through his phony "lush" image. Martin and Sinatra were once playing a foursome of gold in Westchester County with a mobster named Gregory DePalma and the hotel manager of the place where they were appearing. Pretty quickly Sinatra began fretting that DePalma was outdoing Martin and Sinatra, who were, after all, the performers, and should be catered to. When DePalma made three pars in a row before the fifth hole, Sinatra decided he had enough. He drew DePalma aside. "Let me tell you something," he said to the mobster in a low voice. "If you make one more fucking par, or if you beat us, *you* guys will go on the stage tonight, and *we'll* play the lounge."

Sinatra and Martin won the game. Everything was cool.

Martin, known as Dino among his close friends, always sent out red, white, and blue pens at Christmas to his friends, engraved: "It's Frank's world, but he lets me live in it. Merry Christmas. Happy New Year. Dean Martin."

Joey Bishop agreed with Martin about the art of getting along with Sinatra. "We substitute wit for logic," was the way he put it.

On the down side is a Sinatra incident reported by Sidney Skolsky, the Hollywood columnist. "He was leaving [Earl] Carroll's in Hollywood one night with an entourage that included Sammy Davis, Jr., and Sammy's tall, muscular bodyguard. In the parking lot Sinatra became angry because the attendant did not move quickly to bring his car, and when he finally arrived, he did not bring the right car." Sinatra began berating the attendant. "You goddamned dope!" he screamed at him. "You'll do as I say, or I'll have your legs broken!"

"Then," Skolsky wrote, "he ordered Davis's bodyguard to work the attendant over. The attendant suffered a severe beating at the hands of Mr. Humility's [Davis's] hired muscle and later filed a lawsuit against Frank and the bodyguard." Sinatra had his lawyer take care of the mess, and a settlement was reached out of court.

"Frank Sinatra is a fighter," Skolsky wrote. "If he loves you, he goes 'All the Way,' and if you're on his 'All-American Shit Heel list,' he goes all the way too. Sinatra can't hold booze; he gets high very fast and when he gets high, he's a bad boy."

"Whenever I see that big black Dual Ghia coming up behind me," a Los Angeles cabby once said, "I move over fast. I mean, this guy can have people *killed*."

"I know he's spoiled by women," a middle-aged female said. "But if he crooked his little finger, I'd go with him in five seconds."

On a much more serious note, Sinatra continued to defy people who criticized him about his friends among suspected underworld characters. He told Neil Hickey in a 1977 article in *TV Guide,* "I know a lot of those guys. People have said to me: 'Why do you have friends in the mob?' I say: 'I was not *friends* with them.' They said: 'Do you know so-and-so?' I say, 'No, but I've met him.' When the Copacabana was open, there wasn't one guy in show business who didn't meet them. Let them buy you a drink. So I've stopped trying to explain that to people."

Nevertheless, Sinatra's associations with mobsters and other unsavory characters has continued to taint him in the public mind. Frequently there is an almost prayerful sound to defenses of him by his friends. "We've heard these things about Frank for years," Ronald Reagan once said, "and we just hope none of them are true." Thus the image persists of a man who has continued these associations in spite of public disapproval.

Ralph Salerno, a specialist on organized crime who once served with the New York Police Department, wrote about the matter once, in this fashion:

"People say to themselves, 'If Frank Sinatra, who knows presidents and kings, is friendly with Joe Fischetti, Sam Giancana, and all the rest, they can't be all that bad.' That's the service Sinatra renders his gangster friends. He gives them innocence by association. You'd think a guy like Sinatra would care about that. But he doesn't. He doesn't give a damn."

And so Sinatra is an interesting combination of a number of startling opposites, seemingly in endless contention with one another. The genesis of these opposites might be traced to his genealogy. His father was a Sicilian. Sicilians invented brotherhood and camaraderie to the death. The Mafia itself could be said to be an outgrowth of that spirit. Sicily is the home of *omerta,* the law of silence; no Sicilian finks on a friend, or else. . . . Sinatra's mother was a Genoese. Genoa spawned scores of navigators and sailors, adventurers and explorers, including Christopher Columbus. They always seemed to have a kind of longing to plunge into something new, just for the thrill of it.

The Genoese spirit in Sinatra must be in constant conflict with the Sicilian spirit. One struggles for conviviality, adventure, excitement. The other contends for secretiveness, quick anger, blood brotherhood.

The upbeat and manic in Sinatra is the Genoese coming out. The downbeat and the depressive is the Sicilian brooding over fancied hurts, past wrongs, and vengeance. These two strains seem rooted in the essential Frank Sinatra—making him a creature of opposites melded eternally together in constant tension.

Sociologists Patrick Moynihan and Nathan Glazer described Italian-Americans in their work *Beyond the Melting Pot* in this way: "The set of qualities that seems to distinguish Italian-Americans includes individuality, temperament, and ambition. Perhaps the ideal is the entertainer—to give him a name, Frank Sinatra—who is an international celebrity, but still the big-hearted, generous, unchanged boy from the block."

In spite of all the other distractions, it is in music that this "boy from the block" continues to reign supreme. There is much to be said about his continued incomparable skill as a musician, for the way he has been able to adapt his style of vocalizing to cover up the fact that his vocal powers are in definite decline, now that he is in his seventies. Sinatra is still a paragon of technical proficiency. And at an age when the typical opera singer has long since retired, Sinatra continues to produce vocals that are remarkably secure.

His voice, which started out sweet and somewhat adenoidal, became grittier in maturity. Because he no longer has the breath control he once had, he has been forced to intersperse his singing during concerts with solos of instrumentalists and *tutti* band numbers that he sits out. He has cultivated a choppier singing style, one not dependent on his superb ability to phrase and continue to hold a note effortlessly and endlessly.

His phrasing has become "percussively aggressive," in the words of music critic John Rockwell. Sinatra shifted from the smooth, syrupy ballads of the forties to a more jazzy uptempo beat. Indeed his shift to jazzier renditions may have been made to reduce his long-note singing.

Nevertheless, critics have noted that his voice has remained astonishingly the same, with a longevity that could be explained only by his long cultivated natural ease of vocal reproduction. Had he made his name as a belter of lyrics, or a shouter in the style of the hymn wailers, he would have faded long ago—as Elvis Presley did even before his tragic demise. Sinatra has been able to find new ways to cope with his vocal inadequacies. He has, in fact, built into his singing a vulnerability and a fragility that come from his own unsureness about his voice.

Whatever he has been able to do, and however he has been able to do it, he has remained at the top for so long because of one primary reason: an absolute and complete commitment to his art. No matter how much money he made when he was on his biggest rolls, no matter how much fun he wanted to have, no matter how many women he wanted to chase—at no time in his life did he ever let self-indulgence sway his complete commitment to his craft.

In *Playboy* magazine he was once quoted as saying, "You can be the most artistically perfect performer in the world, but the audience is like a broad—if you're indifferent, endsville." And one day in 1963 when he was angry at his son, Frank, Jr., because he thought the young Sinatra was dogging it during a performance, he yelled, "Don't ever let me catch you singing like that again, without enthusiasm! You're nothing if you aren't excited about what you're doing!"

During the years when Sinatra began singing, the pop song par excellence was the ballad. When the crooning phase of popular music declined and the shouters came in, Sinatra's popularity waned. When that happened, he forced himself into other areas of the entertainment business—making movies, appearing in nightclubs.

When rock-and-roll made the romantic balladeer seem passé, Sinatra turned to theme concerts, singing the same old ballads that had been popular when he started. In effect, he was playing to the nostalgia of the people who had been his fans in the past. Later, in the days of hard rock and punk rock, Sinatra continued to release collections of the older ballads, sung in a slightly different way—a way that reflected the age of the singer, and the age of his gradually maturing fans.

Ironically, and pleasantly, the old-fashioned "Golden Age" ballad of the twenties and thirties seems to be making a comeback in the later 1980s. One may be walking down the street or passing a house and suddenly hear the familiar tone of the Sinatra voice, singing in that fine old *bel canto* style, phrasing the words and bringing the ideas of the song to life as only he can.

He has outlasted a lot of men and women who thought they were better than he was. "His interpretations," John Rockwell wrote, "have shaped a half-century of song, transforming creativity into audible reality."

The myth and the man are still at odds. Sometimes the man overrides the myth, and leaves the myth sagging and beaten against the ropes. But at other times the man has stepped up, picked up the myth, and breathed new life and vigor into it.

There is no singer of our time who has invested his music with a wider range of emotion and personal appeal than Francis Albert Sinatra—the man.

And—of course—the myth.

For here, of course, in music, the two combine and coalesce.

BIBLIOGRAPHY

Books

Adler, Bill, with Norman King. *All in the First Family*. N.Y.: G. P. Putnam's Sons, 1982.

Bacall, Lauren. *Lauren Bacall, by Myself*. N.Y.: Knopf, 1979.

Benchley, Nathaniel. *Humphrey Bogart*. Boston: Little Brown & Co., 1975.

Carpozi, George, Jr. *Frank Sinatra: Is This Man Mafia?* N.Y.: Woodhill, 1979.

Clinch, Minty. *Burt Lancaster*. N.Y.: Stein & Day, 1985. N.Y.: Woodhill, 1979.

Davis, Sammy, Jr. *Hollywood in a Suitcase*. N.Y.: William Morrow, 1980.

Davis, Sammy, Jr., and Jane and Burt Boyar. *The Story of Sammy Davis, Jr.* (Publisher unknown)

Demaris, Ovid. *The Boardwalk Jungle*. N.Y.: Bantam Books, 1986.

———. *The Last Mafioso: The Treacherous World of Jimmy Fratianno*. N.Y.: New York Times Books, 1981.

Douglas-Home, Robin. *Sinatra*. N.Y.: Grosset & Dunlap, 1962.

Drosnin, Michael. *Citizen Hughes*. N.Y.: Bantam Books, 1985.

Eisenberg, Dennis, Uri Dan, and Eli Landau. *Meyer Lansky: Mogul of the Mob*. N.Y.: Paddington Press, 1079.

Ellis, George. *Robert Mitchum*. N.Y.: Franklin Watts, 1984.

Exner, Judith, and Ovid Demaris. *Judith Exner: My Story*. N.Y.: Grove Press, 1977.

Flamini, Roland. *Ava: A Biography*. N.Y.: Coward, McCann, 1983.

Frayle, Alan. *Humphrey Bogart*. N.Y.: Exeter Books, 1982.

Gage, Nicholas. *Mafia, U.S.A.* N.Y.: Playboy Press, 1972.

Gehman, Richard. *Bogart*. N.Y.: Gold Medal Books, 1965.

——. *Sinatra and His Rat Pack*. N.Y.: Belmont Books, 1961.

Giancana, Antoinette, and Thomas C. Renner. *Mafia Princess: Growing Up in Sam Giancana's Family*. N.Y.: William Morrow & Company, 1984.

Goldstein, Norm. *Frank Sinatra*. N.Y.: Holt, Rinehart & Winston, 1982.

Greenberg, Howard. *Bogey's Baby*. N.Y.: St. Martin's Press, 1978.

Higham, Charles. *Ava: A Life Story*. N.Y.: Delacorte Press, 1974.

Jewell, Derek. *Frank Sinatra*. Boston: Little, Brown & Co., 1985.

Kahn, E. J., Jr. *The Voice: The Story of an American Phenomenon*. N.Y.: Harper & Brothers, 1946, 1947.

LaGuardia, Robert. *Monty*. N.Y.: Arbor House, 1977.

Mailer, Norman. *Marilyn: A Biography*. N.Y.: Grosset & Dunlap, 1973.

Niven, David. *Bring on the Empty Horses*. N.Y.: Putnam, 1975.

———. *The Moon's a Balloon*. N.Y.: Putnam, 1972.

Pepitone, Lena, and William Stadiem. *Marilyn Monroe: Confidential*. N.Y.: Simon & Schuster, 1979.

Peters, Richard. *The Frank Sinatra Scrapbook*. N.Y.: St. Martin's Press, 1982.

Ranelagh, John. *The Agency: The Rise and Decline of the CIA*. N.Y.: Simon & Schuster, 1986.

Reid, Ed, and Ovid Demaris. *The Green Felt Jungle*. N.Y.: Trident Press, 1963.

Rockwell, John. *Sinatra: An American Classic*. N.Y.: Random House, 1984.

Russell, Rosalind, and Chris Chase. *Life Is a Banquet*. N.Y.: Random House, 1977.

Salerno, Ralph, and John S. Tompkins. *The Crime Confederation*. N.Y.: Doubleday & Company, 1969.

Scaduto, Anthony. *Frank Sinatra*. N.Y.: Michael Joseph, 1976.

Scheim, David E. *Contract on America: The Mafia Murders of John and Robert Kennedy*. Silver Spring, Maryland: Argyle Press, 1983.

Shaw, Arnold. *Sinatra: Twentieth-Century Romantic*. N.Y.: Holt, Rinehart & Winston, 1968.

Shaw, Arnold with Ted Allan. *Sinatra: The Entertainer*. N.Y.: Delilah Communications Ltd., 1982.

Shaw, Artie. *I Love You, I Hate You, Drop Dead!* N.Y.: Fleet Publishing Corp., 1965.

———. *The Trouble with Cinderella*. N.Y.: Farrar, Straus, 1952.

Simon, George T. *The Big Bands*. N.Y.: Macmillan, 1967.

Sinatra, Nancy, Jr. *Frank Sinatra: My Father.* Garden City, N.Y.: Doubleday & Company, Inc., 1985.

Skolsky, Sidney. *Don't Get Me Wrong: I Love Hollywood.* N.Y.: G. P. Putnam's Sons, 1975.

Slatzer, Robert F. *The Life and Curious Death of Marilyn Monroe.* N.Y.: Pinnacle Books, Inc., 1974.

Speriglio, Milo. *Marilyn Monroe: Murder Cover Up.* N.Y.: Seville Publishers, 1983.

Summers, Anthony. *Goddess: The Secret Lives of Marilyn Monroe.* N.Y.: Macmillan Publishing Company, 1985. N.Y.: New American Library/Onyx, 1986.

Talese, Gay. *Fame and Obscurity.* N.Y.: Dell, 1981.

Thomas, Bob. *King Cohn.* N.Y.: G. P. Putnam's Sons, 1967.

Turner, John Frayn. *Frank Sinatra: A Personal Portrait.* UK: Midas Books, 1983.

Turner, Lana. *Lana, the Lady, the Legend, the Truth.* N.Y.: Dutton, 1982.

Wilson, Earl. *Show Business Laid Bare.* N.Y.: G. P. Putnam's Sons, 1974.

———. *Sinatra: An Unauthorized Biography.* N.Y.: Macmillan Publishing Company, 1976.

Windeler, Robert. *Burt Lancaster.* N.Y.: St. Martin's Press, 1984.

Winters, Shelley. *Shelley: Also Known as Shirley.* N.Y.: Morrow, 1980.

Periodicals

"Action in Las Vegas." *Time,* September 22, 1967.

Adams, Cindy. "Frankie Is Still a Real Trouper." *New York Post,* November 10, 1986.

Alter, Jonathan, and Frank Bruni. "Doonesbury Contra Sinatra." *Newsweek,* June 24, 1985.

Anderson, Kurt, and Jay Cocks. "Pop Goes the Culture." *Time,* June 16, 1986.

"At Bogart's Death, a Eulogy for a Tough Guy." *Life,* January 28, 1957.

"At Sea with Sinatra." *Newsweek,* August 23, 1965.

Balliett, Whitney. "Frank Sinatra (Carnegie Hall)." *New Yorker,* October 4, 1982.

"Bee Volant." *Time,* November 10, 1958.

"The Best Defense." *Newsweek,* July 31, 1972.

Block, Alex Ben. "Malibu High; Promoter of Bob Dylan and Frank Sinatra . . ." *Forbes,* October 22, 1984.

"Bogart—Beat the Devil." *Look,* September 22, 1953.

"Bogart—Nite Life of the Gods." *Time,* October 10, 1949.

"Bogart on Hollywood." *Look,* August 21, 1956.

Boulard, Garry. " 'Old Blue Eyes' Does it His Way." *New Orleans,* January 1986.

Braunstein, Bill. "Frank Sinatra: Portrait of an Album." *New Orleans,* March 1986.

Bricker, Rebecca. "Take One (Anecdotes about . . . Frank Sinatra . . .)." *People,* October 31, 1983.

Bryson, John. "Sinatra at Fifty." *Look,* December 14, 1965.

Burns, Cherie. "Frank Sinatra's Heat-Seeking Missive Finds Two New Targets: a Columnist and a Deejay." *People,* May 5, 1980.

Carpozi, George. "The Insane Plot to Murder Frank Sinatra's Producer." *Oui,* November 1983.

"Chairman of the Board." *Newsweek,* October 28, 1963.

Cheshire, Maxine. "Agnew and Sinatra: A Curious Friendship." *McCall's,* May 1973.

Bibliography

Cooke, Alistair. "Epitaph for a Tough Guy." *Atlantic*, May 5, 1957.

Coombs, Al. "Frank Sinatra." *Ladies Home Journal*, October 1979.

"Crooners of a Certain Age." *Chatelaine*, March 1986.

Davidson, Bill. "Life Story of Frank Sinatra." *Look*, May 14, May 28, June 11, 1957.

Eells, G. "Dean Martin: The Man Behind the Myths." *Look*, November 8, 1960.

"Eubie Blake, Frank Sinatra First Inductees into New Entertainment Hall of Fame." *Jet*, September 20, 1979.

Evelyn, Maude. "Idol Remembered." *Esquire*, July 1965.

Ferrer, José M., III. "Sinatra Special That's Very; Sinatra's Spectacular Revisited." *Life*, December 9, 1966.

Fields, Howard. "Sinatra Drops Suit Against Kitty Kelley." *Publishers Weekly*, October 5, 1984.

Fishel, Elizabeth. "Growing Up with a Famous Father." *McCall's*, June 1986.

"Frank Sinatra." *Time*, July 7, 1986.

"Frank Sinatra Returns to a State of Grace with Washington, the Church and Maybe Even Nevada." *People*, February 2, 1981.

"Frankie and His Friends." *Time*, February 5, 1973.

"Frankie and His Stage-Door Johnnies." *Life*, January 1979.

"Frankie in Madison." *Time*, August 25, 1958.

"Fun Couples." *Newsweek*, July 25, 1966.

Gehman, Richard. "Enigma of Frank Sinatra." *Good Housekeeping*, July 1960.

Giddins, Gary. "The One and Only Frank Sinatra." *Stereo Review*, February 1984.

Gittelson, Natalie. "America's Ten Sexiest Men Over Sixty." *McCall's*, October 1985.

Green, Larry. "Restored Chicago Theater Feeds White Way Visions: Sinatra and Black-Tie Celebration." *Los Angeles Times,* September 11, 1986.

Hacket, Pat. "James J. Kriegsmann." *Interview,* May 1986.

Hamill, Pete. "An American Legend: Sinatra at Sixty-Nine." *50 Plus,* April 1985.

Hickey, Neil. "Hardly the Retiring Kind." *TV Guide,* April 16, 1977.

Holden, Stephen. "Guide to Middle Age (Frank Sinatra)." *Atlantic,* January 1984.

"The Hollywood Set and the Kennedy Family." *U.S. News & World Report,* October 16, 1961.

"I Still Love Frank—and I Always Will." *Star,* October 7, 1986.

Joel, Billy. "Frank Sinatra." *Esquire,* June 1986.

Kasindorf, Jeanie. "Republicans at War (Frank Sinatra, Gerald R. Ford)." *New York,* September 17, 1984.

Korall, Burt. "Measure of Sinatra." *Saturday Review,* October 15, 1966.

Martin, Pete. "I Call on Dean Martin." *Saturday Evening Post,* April 29, 1961.

———. "I Call on Sammy Davis." *Saturday Evening Post,* May 21, 1960.

Mathews, Tom, with John Powell. "No Sputum Test for Frank Sinatra." *Newsweek,* February 23, 1981.

Mieses, Stanley. "Sinatra's Ultimate Song (They Did It Their Way)." *Rolling Stone,* November 8, 1984.

Miller, Jim. "Frank Sinatra." *Newsweek,* October 18, 1982.

"My Way *v.* Their Way." *Time,* April 11, 1977.

Neill, Michael. "Chatter (Frank Sinatra)." *People,* July 14, 1986.

Newman, David. "Where the King of the World Goes." *Esquire,* April 1964.

Oulahan, Richard, and Thomas Thompson. "Frank Sinatra Tangles with the Law." *Life,* September 27, 1963.

"Paramount Piper." *New Yorker,* August 25, 1956.

Poe, Richard. "Sinatra OK after Colon Operation." *New York Post,* November 10, 1986.

Pryor, Thomas M. "Rise, Fall and Rise of Sinatra." *New York Times Magazine,* February 10, 1957.

Pyatt, Richard I. "Frank Sinatra—Life in Song." *Encore,* March 21, 1977.

"Render unto Caesars." *Newsweek,* September 25, 1967.

Russell, Rosalind. "Frank Sinatra's $25,000 Weekend." *Ladies Home Journal,* January 1967.

Safire, William. "The Truth about Frank." *New York Times,* September 29, 1986.

St. Johns, Adele Rogers. "Nine Lives of Sinatra." *Cosmopolitan,* May 1956.

Scott, Vernon. "Mia Farrow's Swinging Life with Frank Sinatra." *Ladies Home Journal,* May 1967.

———. "Nancy Sinatra Talks about Life with Father." *Ladies Home Journal,* September 1966.

Shaw, Ellen Torgerson. "Imagine Putting Frank Sinatra and Henry Fonda on Hold!" *TV Guide,* November 7, 1981.

Shipp, Cameron. "Adventures of Humphrey Bogart." *Saturday Evening Post,* August 2, 1952.

"The Sinatra Connection." *Newsweek,* February 5, 1973.

Sinatra, Frank. "Me and My Music." *Life,* April 23, 1965.

"Sinatra." *Saturday Review,* November 25, 1950.

"Sinatra." *Time,* July 31, 1950.

Sinatra, Tina, and Jane Ardmore. "My Father, Frank Sinatra." *McCall's,* December 1973.

"Sinatra Wants More of the Webb Action." *Business Week,* April 11, 1977.

"Sinatra: Where the Action Is." *Newsweek,* September 6, 1965.

Small, Michael. "Chatter (Frank Sinatra)." *People,* August 6, 1984.

"The Story Behind the Photos." *Parade,* November 16, 1986.

Talese, Gay. "Frank Sinatra Has a Cold." *Esquire,* April 1966.

"Talk with a Star." *Newsweek,* July 6, 1959.

Thompson, Thomas. "Seagoing Soap Opera of Captain Sinatra." *Life,* August 30, 1965.

———. "Understanding Sinatra." *McCall's,* October 1974.

Vallely, Jean. "Dean Martin's Closest Friend Is Frank Sinatra." *Esquire,* July 4, 1978.

"The Voice & Payola." *Time,* September 9, 1957.

"Voyage of the *Southern Breeze.*" Time, August 20, 1965.

Weinman, Martha. "Hi Jinks in Hi Society." *Collier's,* January 8, 1956.

Whitney, Dwight. "Frank Sinatra Is Back." *TV Guide,* November 17, 1973.

Wiener, Jon. "When Old Blue Eyes Was 'Red.'" *The New Republic,* March 31, 1986.

"With Sinatra in London." *Newsweek,* November 3, 1958.

DISCOGRAPHY

[List includes only long-playing record albums]

Capitol

Songs for Young Lovers (1954)
Swing Easy (1954)
In the Wee Small Hours (1955)
Songs for Swingin' Lovers (1956)
Close to You (1957)
A Swingin' Affair (1957)
Where Are You? (1957)
A Jolly Christmas (1957)
Come Fly with Me (1958)
Only the Lonely (1958)
Come Dance with Me (1959)
Look to Your Heart (1959)
No One Cares (1959)
Nice 'n' Easy (1960)
Sinatra's Swingin' Session (1961)
All the Way (1961)
Come Swing With Me (1961)
Point of No Return (1962)
Sinatra Sings of Love and Things (1962)

Reprise

Ring-a-Ding-Ding (1961)
Sinatra Swings (1961)
I Remember Tommy (1961)
Sinatra and Strings (1962)
Sinatra and Swingin' Brass (1962)
All Alone (1962)
Sinatra—Basie (1963)
The Concert Sinatra (1963)
Sinatra's Sinatra (1963)
Days of Wine and Roses (1964)
Sinatra—Basie: It Might As Well Be Swing (1964)
Softly, As I Leave You (1964)
Sinatra '65 (1965)
September of My Years (1965)
A Man and His Music (1965)
My Kind of Broadway (1965)
Moonlight Sinatra (1966)
Strangers in the Night (1965)
Sinatra—Basie: Sinatra at the Sands (1966)
That's Life (1965)
Francis Albert Sinatra & Antonio Carlos Jobim (1967)
Frank & Nancy (1967)
Francis A. & Edward K. (1968)
Cycles (1968)
My Way (1969)
A Man Alone (1969)
Watertown (1970)
Sinatra & Company (1971)
Ol' Blue Eyes Is Back (1973)
Some Nice Things I've Missed (1974)
The Main Event/Live from Madison Square Garden (1974)

Trilogy (1980)
She Shot Me Down (1981)

Qwest

L.A. Is My Lady (1984)

Columbia

*Frank Sinatra—The Voice: The Columbia Years,
1943–1952* (6 record set, 1986)

FILMOGRAPHY

Las Vegas Nights (1941) Paramount
Ship Ahoy (1942) MGM
Reveille with Beverly (1943) Columbia
Higher and Higher (1943) RKO
Step Lively (1944) RKO
Anchors Aweigh (1945) MGM
The House I Live In (1945) RKO
Till the Clouds Roll By (1946) MGM
It Happened in Brooklyn (1947) MGM
The Miracle of the Bells (1948) RKO
The Kissing Bandit (1948) MGM
Take Me Out to the Ball Game (1949) MGM
On the Town (1949) MGM
Double Dynamite (1951) RKO
Meet Danny Wilson (1951) Universal-International
From Here to Eternity (1953) Columbia
Suddenly (1954) United Artists
Young at Heart (1954) Warners
Not As a Stranger (1955) United Artists
The Tender Trap (1955) MGM
Guys and Dolls (1955) MGM
The Man with the Golden Arm (1955) United Artists
Meet Me in Las Vegas (1956) MGM

Johnny Concho (1956) United Artists
High Society (1956) MGM
Around the World in Eighty Days (1956) United
   Artists
The Pride and the Passion (1957) United Artists
The Joker Is Wild (1957) Paramount
Pal Joey (1957) Columbia
Kings Go Forth (1958) United Artists
Some Came Running (1958) MGM
A Hole in the Head (1959) United Artists
Never So Few (1959) MGM
Can-Can (1960) Twentieth Century–Fox
Ocean's Eleven (1960) Warners
Pepe (1960) Columbia
The Devil at Four O'Clock (1961) Columbia
Sergeants Three (1962) United Artists
The Road to Hong Kong (1962) United Artists
The Manchurian Candidate (1962) United Artists
Come Blow Your Horn (1963) Paramount
The List of Adrian Messenger (1963) Universal
4 for Texas (1963) Warners
Robin and the Seven Hoods (1964) Warners
None But the Brave (1965) Warners
Von Ryan's Express (1965) Twentieth Century–Fox
Marriage on the Rocks (1965) Warners
Cast a Giant Shadow (1966) United Artists
The Oscar (1966) Embassy
Assault on a Queen (1966) Paramount
The Naked Runner (1967) Warners
Tony Rome (1967) Twentieth Century–Fox
The Detective (1968) Twentieth Century–Fox
Lady in Cement (1968) Twentieth Century–Fox
Dirty Dingus Magee (1970) MGM
Contract on Cherry Street (1977) Columbia
The First Deadly Sin (1980) Filmways/Artanis/
   Cinema Seven

Index

273